The World Before Us

Poems 1950–70

The World Before Us

by Theodore Weiss

Poems 1950-70

THE MACMILLAN COMPANY

COLLIER-MACMILLAN LTD., LONDON

ACKNOWLEDGMENTS

The poem, "The Last Letters," appeared originally
in *The New Yorker*.

Poetry: "The Little Red Book," "A Very
Tokyo," "A Fitting Revenge."

Other poems have appeared in *Pebble*, *The Sewanee
Review*, and *Raffia*.

For Renée

whom I have often wanted—
once or twice begun—
to draw no less than say
in lines of poetry,
though I knew no line
could capture or convey
the quality
that, prompting first
these ventures into verse,
has helped to keep me
at it and to keep me
when all feeling for it
and for every other thing
went flat, stale, awry.
Let it be enough to say
this points, a preface,
to the sketch of you
throughout insinuated
you and I alone can see.
And yet its line
in resonance, in meaning,
and in sweetness
underlines the rest,
the face of you
rising as the moon might
or as Eve
the first time bending
and the last
to bless the flowers,
astonished by her light.

CONTENTS

8

The Catch

1951

The Hook

I

The students, lost in raucousness,
caught as by the elder Breughel's eye,
we sit in the college store
over sandwiches and coffee, wondering.
She answers eagerly: the place was fine;
sometimes the winds grew very cold,
the snows so deep and wide she lost
sight of people. Yes, she was well
satisfied with her work, expected—
while the quarry's owner was
away—to do another year of it.

II

She is hammering. I hear
the steady sound inside our dry
noisy days. Sparks fly; the mind
so taken is mighty for a moment—
quarry and sculptor both; something
caught like love and war in this
golden mesh: and daring caught
that flings like sparks girls
and boys, flagrant cities prompt

to music's will, love and war
its burly seconds.

III

I see again three kids we passed,
three kids lounging at the edge
of a forsaken quarry like something
they had built; in its sleepy pool
they found the whiteness of their bodies,
the excitement like parian marble.

IV

Such the waters we find ourselves
in. We sit in the college store absorbed
in food and talk. Eagerness seizes us
like love that leaves its best sailors
in the mighty waves, love the word
for hook whose catching, and the struggle
there, is our deep pleasure. O the sea
is one great musical clash of minds—
each wave a passion and a mind—
a possessed, tumultuous monument
that would be free.

V

                    We strain forward
as to some fabulous story. Incandescence
springs from her, the hammer of remembrance
fresh, the young woman, bulky graceful body,
face shining, who sculptured all winter
alone near the source of her rock,
digging down into the difficult rock:
the young woman who lost a day once,
talked to her cat, and when the mirror
of her art became too clear, when dreaming

seemed too big for night alone, took long
walks back to people, back to speech,
and time: the woman who at last—
"I do not use live models"—sculptured fish—
"I remember long lonely holidays at shores
when the spray alone defined green shapes
approaching"—has just seen (her eyes
still gleam with the gleam of it,
blink like the making of many
a take) a great catch.

VI

April, we say, is the time
for fish, for reaching in the sea-
like air and the outrageousness of growth
one of earth's original conclusions
like the left-over gill slits
the singing student told us about
in this very spot just two days ago . . .
we are in the middle of a great catch,
there collected as from her year-long
lonely rock, the thrashing clean-
scaled, clear-lit shad in the net.

A Brown Study

by the waters Venus raised . . .

I

Amid ocean of wish—
and the dolphins of whim
with slippery fins flick up
the playful swishing spray
in my comber-briny face—

amid ocean of wish,
shaped no doubt like pineapple, bristling and resolute
on its dish, carapaced
as any crab, crabbed
as any apple can be,
                    amid swirl-
ing and so certain sea (palms
to the right no doubt
as the stalk, saw-toothed,
tusked worthy of a snout, roots

out night-borne chough
chattering as the sea, bruited
from the daysprings of a voice

beyond appeal) with me
the root
      I suddenly see
her rising a resonant, a serene,
the dolphins flipt around her,
pips of spray punctual in eyes
seagreen . . .

II

      I see—
with me the root—her coming,
heart's thump the consequence
as of the fruit that split
           the world.
Through the gape—the parted
lips, the earth upstarting—
dark's naked tread. The bottom-
of-the-deep with all the days deep
sunken crowns pursues.
         Dainty
dreadful step as she that plummeted
come again from earth's fell grip,
winter on her,
        winter
and its whites and, last, maddened
sleep in step: a pomp that holds
the world together worm to star,
orders bedlam in the sky . . .

III

          I see,
and head, pineapple head-
hunter-shrunk, spiked with frowns,
its carapace pricked and scaled,
crossing daggers on all sides,

concentrating studied
brown and bite, racks bitterness
into hardest core of succulence:
rowdy sweet seeing is.
                    Amid ocean
of wish and a leaky day, blue-
botched shadow to this
loneliness, the commotion—
blowing spume like pips—
of my horny notion
                    turns
into her nation, obedient
as waves, bowing whites, vestal—
in devotion, tidy, to the tune—
maidens to the sluttish moon.

Cataract

In the falls, music-woven,
clamorous coils as of cymbals
and shields, I see features
purer than my own: desire
lithe and riding, breaker-bearded,
as the wanderer. I see the first
son of my wish whose thews
were tissued of the sea.

And when my hearing tries
the billows of the wind, back
to its snowy crest and back
to its warring mouth, again I meet
the stranger of myself, the one
that sleeps with restlessness
as the distant mutter of drums
the water cores: in jagged fast-
nesses of fire turmoil strides
one with earth's progenitor.

Astonished, I have seen
the rock that moors these seas;
and I am one with the marching
men, possessed as one, their
dazzled minds obeying potions

of the moon—the ragged lair
of love and hate is one—
the marching men proceeding
by incessant crags, their eyes
reflections of the cataract.

Already gone, the priests
of war, they go to meet themselves, to crash into the center
of the drum, the humming waves,
the fiery rocks where
the sirens of the senses
cold, cold O burning cold
calmly thrum the air.

A Commonplace

as the silly shepherds
after their first radiant scare—
sheep and cattle at their munching
with the winter
                bent yet spin-
ning lilies—forgot . . . hunched
puttering over our benighted star,
we lose track of tears.

See him stamped there,
come down into the common-
place who let himself be stabled
in the blood.
              His walk
brought sea, salt, fish, bread
of his body. Yet within his memory,
each breath travail,

did loiterings of his past,
in sleep perhaps, cajole him: pride,
when as a child he confounded
the learned elders;
                lust:
touched by a woman long possessed,

he knew his virtue troubled
in him;
         or pain itself, simple-
minded pain, did it perhaps reduce
him to the pulse of immediately
suffering man?
               O garden
of agony, so dry it drank his blood,
grew in him, till he cried with a man
mouth and a man mortality . . .

but the garden had its malt as well.
For the shepherds, far inland, blood-
warmed, the star faded into a stone
their cattle sucked for salt.

The Dance Called David

How could I know
how beyond this love
which held me to him and
by its very hold blinded me?

Hours of many days
we walked, past the reputable,
through scenes, people, past
street-names and corners,
                   deep
through poverty with its charming
air of things half-dropping off
into oblivion.
                Words from me,
pointings to bits of color
or surprise longing
urged upon me,
               recalled him
as those that burned in hell
steadied their flames to answer
one earthbound.
             Like something
mattered out of air, a smile—
did it reflect the morning

songs that once enlightened?—
would flicker, then go out.

How could I know,
I who loved him, viewed
the world around us as phrases
visible of his taut unmoving lips,
a music incredible, illuminated
as a battered hurdygurdy
by the love he simply woke,

how could I know
how right I was: windows
strewn behind us, swirling
traffic, parks bouqueting lovers,
children burst from school,
all movements in the meaning
mysteriously clear he was for me.

Only now, years after
his death, do I know what
terror I called friend, what
wrestlings I walked beside, what
anguish—dance of madness, gaiety—
he adorned,
                    the total city
with its grey wizen streets,
each ash-pale puddle, its thin
furtive faces, and the tiniest
broken straw looked after.

Only now I see
how much he deserved—
if love must deserve—whatever
love I could attain, and more,
speechless, ignorant as a child.

These years between, now
that he is with what we are not,
time and the multiple wild fears
have helped me recognize what
first must have frightened
me away.
        Time that cut us
off sharper than space can
holds out again generous hands
as he, the harmonious blacksmith,
leads me through the depths unrolling, these scarred years that are
journeying and pity, of myself.

After Five Years

Beside the lumber
recently cut, some men
struggling up a muddy snow-
ridged road, and five-stories-tall
in your peak-roofed apartment
where warmth was common,

I, after these years
wondrous about returning,
fearful a little,
more than a little hopeful
before the host of possibilities,

I, anxious for revival,
standing at your porthole
window, the latenoon sky
sullen above your sea,
                              ships
puffing along, pedlars,
so that I cannot, do not care
to pursue romantic thoughts
of their cargoes, voyages,
possible great grief,

I, a raveled thread
at the needle's eye, asquint
after the flashing pattern
of my silent partners,

                try hard,
with disappointment, to think
of you spun back, gathered
into your imagery:
                this sky
not yet beginning to ripen
your excellent moon,
the mindless sea
adrift with its abstract boats.

For nothing happens, no north
of thunder scours my hearing,
no lightning hallows my thought
or brightens my conscience,

not even this fruit, here
in this bowl as it used to be
promising incredible secrets,
stirs its full lips
to the words of love
and acknowledgement
we somehow always expected;

not the books where you left
them, dusty, close-mouthed
as the breath we mixed
sometimes beat into a blow

that swirled this room,
crow's nest, back
to first seas breaking,
furious exultant pain.

                    Only
five nameless unshaped men drag
along the turning muddy road
next to the new wood, raw,
awkward, an eye-sore,
five men for the moment
flickering
            (even as flakes
of snow begin to prick the sky-
light we used to praise,
a god's view, so we said,
for our eyes raised)
                    then
slipping—hardly anguish—
through a narrow break
in the grey fence just below;
                    and they are gone.

Shades of Caesar

*Yet Caesar shall go forth; for these predictions
Are to the whole world in general as to Caesar.*

When beggars die, there are no comets seen.

I

Come out into this moment
of clearing and sit on this bench;
come from the files like a man
in the toils, his eyes
hardly his own with staring;

sit and stare, mortuary
for the vine-veined chapel peering,
a battered sundown, through the trees.

We smell the air, do nothing
but smell the air, pungent round
a smoke-shaped bird whose prospectings
echo seconds of the dead:

the ancient scholars
and the ministers-to-be in their solemn
stiff gowns, remembering with bowed

heads in this clearing the Greeks
and the Romans, mixed with the Christian,
muttering dry prayer:
>   disreputable old Rip
Van Winkle bowed at the bias of his spouse's
tongue (we are the solemnity of sleep,
postures flung from the vociferous
game, watching sleep) to overtake
the sport and the peace-piped
Indians:
>   an absentminded wind
from the Hudson no doubt, descendant
of a blow sails once grappled, worries
the leaves in dry-scented eddies

(we do nothing, we who ponder
thieves and bawds, the bountiful
of flesh, trading in need and love,
we the isles bound
by such common trafficking:
>   do nothing
but search the dry shadows under the maple
—maypole once, and after the jubilant
circling, the sugar milked from it
into the guzzling sprawled mouths below—
for the sprawling shape, the long-sleeping
imperial theme—call it thyme—of myth)
the leaves that are falling
>   and
>   falling
round and round like charred days
ript from the calendar
of what a leaf or two ago
seemed endless:
>   O fierce felicity,
the air gross with diadems,
sleek-headed sounds and winds,
ritual like nude runners,

                        the seed
of darkness a relentless fertility
whose holy touch, we thought,
a feast of shepherds, would enable us
to strike off the sterile curse

(how in the fields, peasant
as rain and wind, the hours
of light have labored;
now light pauses
before the hail and the fire,
mountain of fire that sinks
into the sea)
                falling
                        and
                                falling
deeper and deeper till we drown.
Now amid the swaying
leaves-and-light
                        (the city
near us, come in like a wind's
mixed murmurs, caught in its commerce,
unaware of the sickness welling
within it;
                yet despite all complaints,
all obvious omens, the people remain:
the sociable beast, the terrible
touching,
                a hospitality
for strangers and songsters: the blind
man groping toward us, singing
into the noises, cuts a path

through dowagers and worn men, veterans
from new wars done with life, boys
and unwedded girls, children
exposed, a wilderness like autumn
awaiting the big wind.

The towers
of their worship around them, I toss
till flickers of my first
stream appear,
                    those presences,
the Little Lehigh, lounging a long
distance from the lofty Hudson, counting
over and over the wealth of that sun-
squandered day, the hot grass
and prickly slum of air
like a strew of new senses.
                                        Heavy
boughs canopy waves coiling mid-
forest: satyrs these flashing
cars and burled faces,
melancholy party of pleasure
avid to be the burst of flame
and the sovereign of ruin
chaired on the sun's shoulders)
                                        we drowse,
till I think of the burning and the brevity:
thirty years now and at least half
eaten away
                    (*when I consider that Alexander
at my age had conquered so many nations
and I have done nothing memorable,
have I not just cause
to weep?*)
                    shall I, in this drowsy
campus, with the rest having forsaken
all colors, in coward's pride
—neither cold nor hot—
denying the garden's strength
of knees,
                    shall I—these limbs
that looked sturdy, longer
than time, consumed
by slow flame—

not even climb
(in the camp of Mars, Venus and Mars
intertwining), a wiry wind-conspiring
smoke expanding into huge air—
wind Shelley forged, blasting tyrants:
"Look on my works, ye Mighty, and despair!"

and Milton's storm, rooted
in the Muses, inspired by his passion,
that, driving two ways, cleared
the sky of corruption, blew down
the devil's horde, evil's harvest—
                              hinging
a blue god-lunged blast? . . . nothing
shall burgeon from these limbs?

II

Caesar, had the knives
not dressed him with generous wounds
like imperial autumn, not done him
kind service of cutting him down
at his *floruit*,
                  would have seen
his vision dwindle, surrounded
by the abiding faces, unctuous, meek,
of betrayal—and broad, brightest
above them all, his own—
                        he who pushed
his name and his terror to the outposts
of barbaric speech, towns swept
together, till the world seemed
a province of Rome.
                    (He was only
the latest, the last, and the loftiest
wave of that tide and that city
that might, had any one money
enough, be bought, for a time.)

At last violence had found
its dandy.
        But what of those legions,
forces pride and success little
prepare for, gathering
as they winter within him?
               Unabated
the sly stream flows on, the one
that first exalted him. His vision
drowned, he would have stumbled
on to absentmindedness,
his former greatness, a stream
of mirrors,
           mockingly sinuous
before him: Cleopatra
(snug in his best friend's arms)
the barge a blaze of motion, in her
eyes new beckons of conquest
              (*could they,
the never-daring, know, they who called
her serpent, Circe, whore, what splendor
sped in her toils?*)
          the river,
were it Lethe, eyed by her,
caught on the point of wonder,
would forget itself forever
in her memory!
        (*how she came
to me in that troubled dusk, the ships
burnt behind me, hemmed in on that island,
mind overburdened with schemings:*
               *my bed
untouched, tucking my gown around me,
I paced the tower: how, wrapt
in a flock-bed*)
        proper vehicle
for one of her craft
           (*bound like mere*

merchandise, she came: emerging, she fell
before me, raised eyes and a sight
I never dared admit:
                    years and years'
march along the scarred dusty body,
past Mars mighty in our bravest fight,
past his most manly nakedness
upon another front, in different
arms, suddenly to emerge
                         into air
a site of thyme, the fabulous breadth
of childhood like a god buried deep
in the heart.
              My battles, those past,
those recruiting me? Her beauty, her dark
brow bright with long-rooted eyes,
caparisoned rivers and trees.
But what charm was hers let a year—

winter it was, winter within the walls
of a well-provided sly enemy,
and only a handful of men by me:
I trusted to the report of my exploits:
was I expected to anticipate this?—
                              kitchen
conspiracies and vast conquest idling,
nations put by and moldering armies
attest.
        Death itself to our solemn
employment, the roaring engines
of our siege, yielded its passion,
a pure torrent I, confounded, could
only submit to)
                seven years Calypso
kept Odysseus by her, seven years
coiled in the golden loom
of her hair and her spell-weaving
body:

        despite his unbroken lament
by the sea, moments, cogent beauty,
must have held him—
                as the Nile
winding—the sly stream flows on—
its mysterious and redolent
source, headlong over his triumphs.

And no issue or comment
came of this year as he zealously
carried the empire past the known
world
           (*beauty was terrible, too much*
upon us, sheer terror; and terror at last,
denying desire, arresting hate, dictated
an end)
            even we realized
something of what he saw in her;
what was our clumsiness
but the rough side of the silken
feelings she spun within us
                  (*my roots*
held, the first voices, the very forces
she summoned out of me; let a woman—part
divinity though she be—dangle and dungeon
me with a shiny hair?
                And how retire
from the world I labored to build? What
empire can one pluck from dalliance?
Man and the universe were
my specialty.
             Hers also, angling
to satisfy her mildest caprice;
like kittens my men tumbled around her!
man sucked in as by the sea. How long
could any man's back show above this
whimsical will?)

                    the sly stream
flows on . . . those few that grumbled,
protested him caught, we dangling
with him, by an old salt fish,
were jealous or impotent; we saw
what a battle our general had
on his hands.
                    But we, being
what we were, forgot what he was,
what he had done. Forget the capitol
of Rome?
                    We could drown our wounds,
our women, all the towns we spoiled
in a cup of wine; not Venus herself,
though he went where love's wars
waged thickest, could distract him
long from ambition.
                              His cleverness
did not fail him, his awareness
of facts: his age, his nature
(hardly cut out to be an Antony),
the price of such pleasures.
So let us say a year was
an heroically short time,
                              nothing
he cared to entrust to the public
page beside the Civil Wars: a year
dismissed, as his whole private life
would be by the future—
                              absentmindedness,
his own as well as the world's:
one day an old man scarcely
thought of . . .
                    yet we loved him;
all his honors and riches—
the vast delicate loot—he shared
equally with us.

Enormous debts
he incurred for the people.
Bribery? Old frost-faced Cato
himself admitted that in a time
like ours bribery under certain
conditions was for the public good.

Consider the excess common
in our city, taken for granted.
How many really objected
to the war, any war?
                    Only he
looked after us. The same diet
he had of hardships and dangers,
avoiding no labor.
                    Not that he
pampered us, hardly! He had us
marching days and nights without
stop in all kinds of weather
and enemy country, this
before battle!
                    We loved him,
his shifts of temper, his quickness,
his Herculean acts. An example
he was of what we—soldiers
common enough, good
with a spear, liquor, women—
could be and in him were . . .

an old man scarcely thought of;
then as history, futility;
not even hated or envied;
victories forgotten, doubted
(*my own or somebody else's?*)
by spittle betrayed, by gout.

Who knows his motives—
any better than he did, ambitious

and the ambition of the mob, moving,
moved, the people his sons
and his sires.

        Only what he thought
he was—the sly stream flows on—
still alive, snatched out of his
palsied hands,
           he pushed aside
by the glittering, arrogant, ruthless
young man of himself straining
forward and upward, the world
before him and he ahead
of the whole world,
             pushed aside
like a thing for the nursery.

Better for him, than the slow
blades met in the ambushes
of flesh, embrace of a Cleopatra
he could not outwit:
         death (*a sudden
one*) unexpected, yet a death earned,
made with his own hands, body
hacked by knives he recognized.

Let a bosom-friend (*O traitor,
what dost thou, thou my son?*) batter
death's door, Charon him,
the salt crust of sorrow clamped fast
in his jaw, over the last stretch
(the stream flows on)
           like the Rubicon
—at his delay a noble-faced stranger
appeared out of nowhere, piping.
Soldiers and trumpeters (I was one
of them) flocking around him,

our general snatched a trumpet
from one, ran to the river,

and sounding advance, plunged in,
saying, "Let us go whither
the omens of the gods
and the iniquities of our enemies
summon us. The die is cast."

Like children or birds quick
for the falconer's call we followed.
Are omens not to be obeyed—
into Lethe and into the dark
continuous wood: into his own
blood-finished monument.
                    He, last
heart of this bloody wilderness,
struck, became a tumult
of mouths,
          his last will
and long-lasting testament
(the wound in his loins was fertile):
all his wealth, palaces and arbors,
torments and fervors, he left
to us.
      For such a one
should hands that bore deaths,
victories, delights, love bursting
violent leaves as summer hived
in the seed then,
             not torch
to demonstrate amid the seethe
of honey poured through roaring
civil cracks (O sociable beast!)
the imponderable dark stalking
the palsied streets?

III

           Fittingly the blow-
crowned, arms outstretched,

climax in the royal line, returns
us to a denouement of Caesars: such
the diverse will of an age's lust:

returns as the wheel must,
as the season; one role
a mask for the other: one aimed
at heaven, the other hanged
by the heels, cut down lest they
wither on the bough; in this rack
all crimes ecstatic.
             "Those we raise,
risen too high, we seek to humble:
see, he bleeds, is mastered
by such straits as the meanest
carpenter hews his life to.
             Great men,
time's motley, exceed our need:
consider the lilies of the field,
the common unnamed leaf.
             Men, rifled,
the mines dug up against themselves,
founded and scummed and blown
into the base—battlement,
tower, a kingdom-
come—of war."
             This is the way
they redeem themselves, the way
a Caesar charms them:
one moment out of the mire,
the luminous moment becomes a halo
of hate, their knives and faces
flashing.
             O melt all beggars
into the bold bright image—the die
is cast—of Caesar: pour them
(Rome enough) into tribute

of a comet:
                    such a thing is Caesar.

                        IV

We wake, our sleep a falling
mire of faces, a ring and a rack,
the taste of our father strong
in our mouths, sting of his death
upon us, we who bore him
                            and denied
him, who bore him and broke him,
hating the love he demanded,
the death he proved for us.
Hate is the bright sword
that reflects faces crooked.

What light of noon—the betrayer's
smile gold for it—can tell those who
killed Caesar from those who chaired him?

When we adore love, hate stabs us;
fallen before hate, the dove
impales us . . .
                    was the morning
so different after the killing
of Cock Robin, the babes
in the wood, the apple whose
bite split earth into serpent pain?

                        V

We, are we not equipt with faculties,
with hands, hearts ("slight he was,
subject to attacks and fits
of all kinds of weakness") equipt
for the labyrinth as the best of them?

Did we in our time not also hang one,
his mistress beside him, one we prized
first ("we were Caesar's fortune;
he used us, leather, mortar, iron,
battering rams . . . we loved him,
with groans were willing")
                                confounded
in doubts (*better than a long life*
of trembling a sudden death
and a noble one) cowardice
come to manhood within us

("is it so much worse, eating
roots like tumors, drinking
horse-piss and rotting water
that shows us beasts, than living
with old inescapable fears?")
                                What good
hiding in the mountains or rushing
home from the fields? what sanctuary
the world-husking kiss
                        (*behind us*
stood the Ethiopian Mountains
of the Moon where the Nile issued,
whispers of the undiscovered country,
and the creatures of Isis)

where the heart is, there the muses,
there the gods sojourn, a great
guest in small houses!
                        O heroes,
shall one moment of oblivion overcome
centuries of striving, pervert all valor?

Appetites—bitter teeth
of beasts the air, fanged poison
the dust and the sea—
grope for shapes.

This our nakedness, our secret
lust, come to embrace us.
                              All men,
breathing as one, bound in one
brotherly season of fear
and hate, in the late
sun falling together,
                              mere son
of man, our hope and hate putting
greatness on you, Caesar, govern us
with the whore you espoused. Very glorious
the city sits in the midst of the seas
worshiping lust
                              ("age cannot wither you . . .
for vilest things become themselves in you,
that the holy priests bless you
when you are riggish")
                              hear midnight
streets dizzy with drink, mob of stinking
breath and sweat, loudest at the gates
welcoming chaos;
                              what sheaves
are these, what unity of desolation?
Into great waters your pilots have
brought you, O city; your fairs
are heaped, riches sacked from every
cranny of the world:
                              stumps, like the garden
trim with murder, loom as this proud
bloodclot city
                    ("how the towns
and the suburbs, shaken, would flee
you they yesterday craved, you
sinking into the sea's midst")

of execration, Caesar's last province.
Alexander, the Greeks said, went as far
as chaos. Have we—faculties, wishes—

not pushed beyond! . . .
                              those of us
that shall survive this, cowards, awed
by all things as by ourselves
(neither hot nor cold) die
a thousand deaths;
                        see the core storm
in the robin, perhaps the hardiest
heroism of all, wounds so daily-
constant through their interstices
awareness oozes as through a muffled
fall.
        Odysseus at the end,
recalling his toils, the mad
stream he had ruffled, shed
ambition, divine loves,
immortality,
                and through the ruddy
weather of wound and time sought
a private life and, the sea
settled, oars taken for scythes,
a kindly death.
                        What better,
amid the sudden flare-up
of berries like trophies
of one's own fabulous past,
than to sit on a mound
                        watching
the goat at its shaggy song,
the tragedy so deep around
one is completely part of it,
apart like faun and goat
from history,
                like old Rip
listening to those Catskills,
swift-footed mountains of time
moving more subtle than clouds,
the sly Hudson, leaves . . .

in honeycomb
noon, like women around, they led
out the songs (daily words once)
from cloud and brook
by like strings, the music
of the small folk and the dances:

in the waters of that falling
melody many faces shone,
time itself idling there
where the suns drink, one broad-
faced Dutch interior . . .
twenty years,
thirty, we wake from our dreams
of the mountains, gradually
leave the green knoll,
the lordly Hudson,
steeped in a purple cloud, a sail
like a drop of sleep aerial on it,
losing itself in the color-quick
highlands;
pass the heady blue melt-
ing into apple green, into grey vapors,
our joints rusty as the shining fire-
lock we started out with
(from roaring
mountain cataract to rutted river bed,
the sly stream flows on); push
through the tangle of birch, sassafras,
witch-hazel,
out into the city,
into strangeness, a snarling of dogs,
stiff row after row of houses, familiar
haunts of maples and sun once, files
staunch against noon.
Yet forest-
muffled, midway, the wistful faces

of old desires peering at us, there are
clearings;
                         hidden in the shadiest
shabbiest tree there are boughs
buoyant with foliage all gold:
                                        these daily
streets, the church like a rock
shattering dawn, the young woman
bountiful of flesh, lofty on high
heels, her painted features
turned to the sun,
                         prefaced by sparrows
bathing delicately in dung.
Their loves are private.
                              But who now—
no interstices to slip through,
the jealous blows coming
closer and closer—shall know
contentments of such privacy?

                                   let me go
down, down to the bottom of my people's
bestiality and doom; there on the sodden
floor let me grovel, dire mien

of their dreaming. The gods,
whoever they are, are ruthless,
unforgiving, taking the full pleasure
of their punishment however

we turn. What difference what
goddess Paris preferred; his end
would have been the same. All we can
do—our dignity—is decide

who shall kill us. Let me,
with my people, spurning the one
talent I have, pull down the temples
and palaces. Then at last

the gods will warm us; winter
we can by their ruinous burning

                              smashed
the gadgets between us and what we are,
the desert of the sociable beast flooded
by the ravenous tide, wide as wind
and snow, of the senses,
                    self's animal
breaks loose: the gardener of prayer,
the hero of praise: the wisdom
in tooth and claw and fang:
                        in voracious
rose, sweet-tooth, and the berries
strewn like mouths in the grass,
fang-light and the sea: the star
apart, by strangeness taken in.

Licking honey from the murderous paw,
out in the open, reason made
commodious,
                only then peace
like stone (the lion hot within)
a rising chapel of stone, is reached
again: around it, desolate earth its pit,
by the roseate window of sun-up, the flesh
of apple and peach, of burgeoning limbs.

Outlanders

1960

Preface

"Sonja Henie," the young girl,
looking out of the evening paper,
cries, "just got married!"

"I don't care if she did,"
the mother replies. "She's been
married before; it's nothing new."

Darnel, Ragweed, Wortle

And turning to me, the young poet
tries to say once more what weeds
mean to him—
                luscious weeds
        riding high, wholly personal:
        "O go ahead, hack away as much
        as you like; I've been thrown out
        of better places than this"—

his face just come back from staring
out the window into a day
wandering somewhere in early fall
and a long quiet contented rain,

the sky still on his face, the barn
out there, green-roofed and shiny,
gay in a wet way with its red
wet-streaked sides.
                    I read his poem,
mainly about how much it likes weeds,
how definite they are, yet how hard
to come by.
              I say, "Like all the rest
only their own face will do, each
a star squinting through 30,000 years
of storm for its particular sky."

And as though a dream should try
to recollect its dreamer, we look out
across the long highways of rain,
look out

          Darnel, Ragweed, Wortle

I do not say what we both are thinking
as we see it flicker in that rain-
soaked day: the face exceeding
face, name, and memory,
yet clinging to our thoughts.
                    Black
against the sky, a flock of cranes
shimmers, one unbroken prickly rhythm,
wave on wave, keeping summer jaunty
in its midst.
     And Sonja Henie,
the star, the thin-ice skater,
after many tries, tries once more.

"The poem's not right. I know,
though I worked at it again and again,
I didn't get those old weeds through.

I'm not satisfied, but I'm not done
with it yet."

There in that wheatfield
of failures, beside all manner
of barns, frost already experimenting,
the slant of weather definitely
fall, lovely scratchy

Darnel, Ragweed, Wortle

Barracks Apt. 14

All must be used:

this clay whisky jug, bearing
a lamp-shade; the four brown pears,
lying ruggedly among each other
in the wicker basket; the cactus
in its pot; and the orange berries,
old now as they dangle from their twigs
as though badly hung there.

These as well as the silence,
the young woman reading Aristotle
with difficulty, and the little girl
in the next room, voluble in bed:
"I'm talking in my sleep . . . laughing
in my sleep . . . waking in my sleep"

all are parts hopeful, possible,
expecting their place in the song;
more appealing because parts
that must harmonize into something
that rewards them for being, rewards
with what they are.

                    Do this and do,
till suddenly the scampering field
you would catch, the shiny crows
just out of reach, the pears
through which a brown tide breaks,
and the cactus you cannot cling to
long like that thorny Aristotle
suddenly, turning, turn on you

as meaning, the ultimate greenness
they have all the time been seeking
in the very flight they held
before you. No matter what you do,
at last you will be overwhelmed,
the distance will be broken,

    the music will confound you.

The Greater Music

All things turned to Orpheus' hand.
Narcissi bloomed—and all at once—
the burning loveliness far underground,
then bloomed a retinue of bees, all hived

as in a greater self, intent on hearing
the sweetness of their lives, stilled
in that welling strain; and animals,
rapt as plungings of the sea,

admired in that pellucid glass
what they might be. But only Orpheus,
when the fierce hand plucked his strings,
could not consent to the divisions

of the lute. His breath, greeting
the stone-deaf, eager stones (though why
those fury-flying stones did not hear
and build into a tower of hearing

round his air I cannot tell), delighted
to be ript and strewn like tortured
peace out of that terrible grip,
too rhapsodic for the mortal ear.

Yet as his head drifted down the stream,
the waters touched by that perfect lip
at once were set to dreaming, his course
the music they drank as from a golden cup.

A Gothic Tale

Framed by our window, skaters, winding
in and out the wind, as water reeling
so kept in motion, on a glittering
edge spin out a gilded ceiling.

Fish, reflecting glow for glow,
saints around the sun, are frozen
with amazement just one pane below.

Skates flash like stars, so madly
whirling one can hardly tell which
is sky and which the watery floor . . .

one night two strait-laced couples,
a footman over them, rode out
in a dappled-horse-drawn sleigh
onto the river, a moonlit lark.

The ice broke and they—sleigh,
footman and all—riding in state,
rode straight on into the lidded water.

That winter all winter folks twirled
over them who—framed in lace,
frost the furs, the shiny harness

and their smiles the fire that keeps
the place—sat benignly watching.

"One foot out, one foot in,
are we real," thought one, "we who
wander sheepishly in dreams, or they,
the really sleepless eyes, under us?

And every night who knows (a laughter
troubles us like dreams) who skates
(a thousand watch-fires the stars)
above, peering through the pane?"

This Narrow Stage

But who is this, what thing of sea or land?
Female of sex it seems,
That, so bedecked, ornate, and gay,
Comes this way sailing, . . .

Asia on the one side,
Afric on the other, and such divers
under-kingdoms that the actor,
coming in, must ever begin
with telling where he is?

The first scene surely
needs no wordy explanation:
three Ladies strolling together
to gather flowers, a matter of May
seasons in their hands;

each thing in its kind
sheltered under revery's wide
eyelids, we seem to tread the verge
of song, every daisy meadows,
that time's mad rivers are

bemused. But by and by,
and in the same place, we hear

news of shipwreck: distraught shape,
the turmoil and the horror proud—
to reach such gentle apex—

in its eye; hit by darts
wilier than his, salty Neptune,
tossing in storm crowning his storm
and flung to mortality's shoal,
drowns in its sweetness.

Can airs from Ladies,
swelling though their skirts
may be, and sighs from ruffled seas
so intermingle? Yet what unities
have we but circumstance

must grant them? Ladies
are persuasive; shipwrecks bear
their own important cargo. But when
the one bedecks the other (fair
plumes and perfumes giddy

with the stir) hard put
indeed each player is to tell—
himself as well as others—where he
stands, the many under-kingdoms
wrangling for their chance

upon this narrow stage, Asia
on the one side, Afric on the other.

Simples of the Moon

I

Deride as much as you will
late shadowy walks in Bronx Park.
Spiked railings and stone walls,
crumbling like a chalky skull,
cannot long suppress the will

of a seed. Like you,
Albert Ryder (the thin caul
of a wide-eyed moon between you
and the city, and a field, going
greenly on, its music abysmal,

massive, warm), slipt out
between newspapers, a codfish,
a dried bread, partly decomposed
mice snug in their traps,
a lopsided pot simmering all day.

II

These you lived by,
even as you studied inchworms—
any perch for saunters in the air—

from windows in your workshop,
shaggy-browed two casements

commanding an old garden,
kept going by some great moon-
time making trees, shadowing you
like the cat, nine-lives-cosy
in a fork, till things

entered—the wind, the wind,
the wind—that you could see.
Demeanors of the mind they were,
less than the faun scaring
the graces, spicy wanderings

III

like faun and flavor
of some violin, yet instinct
with a valor, innocent of failure,
taking any air as able to endure,
a passion equal to all hope.

Homecoming

Like that oldtimer who has kept by me
I know the place of danger and of change
and most, most tellingly, when they jut forth
their avid face, the moments that deny me
a staple of the place.
                              That oldtimer—
rope bloody through his hands, coursing
as the cordage sings: dog's lope and grace
of the deer, faun like a woman's love,
meat-scent fattening whatever air;

that song also like his chambered bow,
twenty years' music coiled waiting within,
catching on comrades, harnessed together,
winter and summer caught in the toils,
driving the sun, from east to west
one wheaten swath, his goddess winged
in this weather;
                        love likewise enduring
(twenty years not able to take its measure,
not chimerae, not orgies, able to make it
forget) its own lulls and forgettings,
surges of hunger the sea shrinks away in—

that oldtimer, buffeted as he was,
gripping twisted planks in a rampant sea,
clutching the last shreds of his wits
against rock and brackish brutality,
saw still this was his native element.

II

This and not sea-nymphs, not floating
islands centered in a season made of wish;
not noon with air the tissue of a voice
winsome at its loom,
                spinning out
along the ample warp of boughs a spell
that tangles men like thrushes in a net,
knots them, fawning claws or bristle set,
in one appetite.
              Like him mast-pinioned,
flung by stormy words out of the sea,
hot blood in the lungs of a blinded cry
or grist for a bird song they become;
but only his ears open to homespun hunger—

"feasts and vistas of love, the struggle's
gaiety: her voice in all its changes,
in division strongest, ranging over peaks
and losses, leaf-tossed island in her voice"

(like him golden liar she was, lyre
strummed for their amusement by the gods,
loom too in its weaving night and day,
spinning him nearer home)
                "in our room
the changes come, zodiac in its restless
pride, its creatures here to suck selfhood
from our interbreeded breath;
               she the sea
under me, dolphins arch a sleek summer

by our side, the poplar and the birch
whirled in their autumn"—

III

                rooted, yes,
as his old tree, but flowering in open love,
in boughs that branch a household, season
air and crown, as it is crowned, sky-
high change.
           In the top-greenery
the gods, looking down, dumbfounded,
at our strangeness with vast unblinking
incredulous eyes,
               envy us that we forever
change and, by our changing, settle
in this whirling place.
             Better driftwood
swirling in the sea, an olive's litterings
over a battered body, than the ample warp
of boughs that snags us—thrushes in a net—
out of the complicated, mortal text.

In This Tower

As the sycamore makes one thing
of the wind, and the birch another . . .
as these roses, four kinds of roses,
related in scent, yet as different
as their colors, make in the vase
out of their difference one fragrance . . .

so in your moods by the gamut
of glances, the narrow yet infinitely
many diapason of breath, you make
one sundry thing of the air. And I
by the strength of my senses, great
folly of love that will lead me

whence the hardihood of its caprice
desires, I dare it, this one sundry
thing of the air. And I hold it
within me as I move in the clear
bewilderment like mirrors of its mansion
as the sycamore—its hackles tingling,

deepening with the scent it is
bringing out of itself in the wind—
moves through the wind that radiantly
moves inside it. Linger, I cry,

in this tower, improvised as the flare
of my breathing, as the patterns

sheaved of the birch and the sycamore
in the curious wind, in this headlong
tower of my tuning, this valorous air
that swells through me, bowers round
for the person of you it supports,
enlarged in the song you sing forth.

So moved, I would hold you,
a racing—the leaves more fluttered
than fauns—as of trees deeply rooted,
clouds anchored, massive, ever moving,
the mountains are, I still at last
in the tempest birch- and sycamore-bruited.

A Local Matter

I

But who does us?
Who flexes like fingers, strains
in our sinews that they sing,
one felicitous agony?
These thoughts, these thoughts
thieving through night that things—
even hope and lust everlastingly
raucous—heckling locals
trying to distract us,
fall dumb.

II

The cat all evening
lulled the mouse, licked it
and pricked it and loved it that
never a moment did it move
out of sight. O the success,
the bliss, the fittingness
of nature there; mouse
recognized its consummation, its all-
devoted, all-devouring heir,
where the future was

suddenly breathless.
Grin, claws.

III

Hum of mouths within me:
waters at their loom spinning
out the sea, the lilies
in their velvet skill break
stones, break stems for a somewhere-
rooted, roar-cored wind.

IV

And you, enchanting
the maddest din as winter
pears can pipe the speckled curves
in scented air of summer round,
do you not, like that lady
of the wild things, discover
in your bending
wells, a company of drinkers
borne up by the swell?

V

These the lines
I do not somehow have
to learn; they find their parts
at the moment of burning:
the appropriate pain, the fitting
grief. Meantime I cling
to things that belong:
shag-root of a dog
not the whole world can impress,
the sparrow tucked in the sky
ticking out fall.

VI

And yet the subtle
strings twang into us all;
I think of turtles in a bowl,
their shells like painted shields,
churning upon one another,
each overwrought by private music,
rushing together to one
gleaming doom.

VII

Now in the lute-time,
soon brute, of the year I
slouch down, the silky lounge
of one in perfect health
(hear the chestnut
gayly crying in its country fire).
I lounge as I wait the advent
of one all sinew and strain,
the lunge. Like a string tautening
to the discords of precisianist
pain, I fit: come, windy
dark, like all the kingdoms
of the North and within the gates
of my Jerusalem set your sundry
singing thrones!

VIII

In the state of weeds,
high-spirited undergrowth,
there congregate vast dynasties.
Themselves flashing armor and plume
before the shadow coming on
of the long summer light, locusts
clash their cymbals.

Again and again, mighty in leaves
as Nimrod, the mouse enters
that the seasons be maintained
as locally as a broken fence
beside a yawning dog,

IX

till I, skinned,
glistening, one of many
hides racked in a row, lesser
tale in a larger, from the lean-
to of noon, sink to mouse, catgut,
fiddlings of some nameless bog.
At work religiously, maggots welcome
me passing through, good will
from one end of death to the other,
into and through that minerals
know me, the odors use me;
how the hum becomes me,
once and ever the household
word of the air.

An Egyptian Passage

Beside me she sat, hand hooked and hover-
ing, nose sharp under black-lacquered hair,
and body, skinny, curving over a brownish big
thick book.
        I glanced past her hand to pages
she checked; there, beside strange symbols,
curious hawk-beaked little birds at attention,
gawky beasts, stiff plants, some more than strange,
set next to words which I, despite the rail-
yard shuttling shadows and the battering light
at the end of the tunnels, gradually made out
as items in a German-Egyptian lexicon.

Then red- and black-brick tenements; billboards;
excavations; three boys with mattocks, digging
by a squat, half-finished, bushy hut;
tumbled-together shacks, drifting in the way
of winter; near the bank, its wharf rotted
through in several places, a gutted house
like something done by fire, slowly floating
(so it seemed) out on the river; smoke stacks;

and the dumps, one burning in three spots,
lurid like old passion among heavy piled-

up boxes and black banged-in pots, and birds
floating above like ashes.
       Birds too
on the Hudson: ducks in strict formation,
gulls—like lungs—working their great wings
or perched like dirty, jagged lumps of ice
on the ice caking the shoreward waters,
till another dump, a vast flattened white,
for the train's racing flapped into the air.

And all fashion of ice, from shoots in spray
to zigzag rows, waves at their climbing's apex
trapped, frizzled work, to tesselation.

Along the shore a shaggy red-brown brush,
so thick partridges must be crouching in it,
as in the Hudson, under an icy lid,
a brood of clouds. And heavy-headed, long,
thin, flaggy things like the stuff we think of
growing beside the Nile.
       The trees bare,
through them the early light already deepened,
purpling. And rocks rode through, by speed
light as the distant hills, the clouds, crumbling,
fitful, round them.
      Like the little crate-
white houses across the river, quiet enough,
but indoors, I knew, no bush for its morning
birds busier.
      Still her eyes never left
the ibises that fluttered under her fingers.
Deeper and deeper she went, like the sun
unfolding fields, forsaken spots, and towns,
the dirty sharp details of, always more
and always clearer—like the river itself,
the roads agog with golden high-legged going,
song-sparrows swept from their nests, their wings
praising the sun—the steeples, broken houses

and smoky streets, kids dashing in and out
of hide-and-seek, the billowy wash on lines.

And I thought of sitting on a polar star
a million miles away, looking down at this earth
surrounded by its tiny nimbus of a day.
And I saw the days—each hour a speck, twelve
motes combined—like waves like sparks like bushes
burning, lined up one by one, for its intricate
strokes each a kind of word.
                              "Poughkeepsie,"
the conductor said as he took her ticket
from the seat. Several times he tapped her
on the shoulder before she looked up, fumbled
for her coat and bag, and lurched out.

Descent

At least another time believed
there was an age more golden,
golden age when men could move
the raging beast, the stolid oak,
and rocks like notes upon a lip.

Yes, it believed earth, flame
and river, vying, in reflection
of ceremony-charmed and -charming
mates forgot their differences.

Even time, through woods
and wilderness of cities, down
to the dark iron rungs of death,
forgot. Grief humming, agony saw
itself in another light. So far
music swelled.

II

Another time
believed . . . and what discovery

74

was here, those great first days
in woods, in wall-eyed back bed-
rooms, your lips a live coal
to my mouth, warbling
holy, holy, holy,
                    O my Adam
and O the glory that thronged
our wayward dingy dangling town,
each dawn a steeper mountain-
top for the night's deep-
ening climb.
                In your hands
songs so erudite they found out
the lordly dances, olive branches,
of my body.
                Kings and queens
like owls and cardinals stood by,
royal lovers, the jealous dead,
that we should have found out
their sovereign secret and come
abed to their godhood, to lie
in such fixed state.

                    III

                Generations
of martyrs rose, a Francis
shining, hymned hawk-eyed songs
pining to compose the world—

nothing of old, no cold, no wind
or hail or snow, not flailing sea,
not brokenness could withstand
the slight smooth wield
like a long light
                flying,
wild bird crying, of your wrist—

to compose the shattered world
into one field of love.
                    O strew
these backroom beds with violets
and rue; fill them with rumpled
cries as of creatures thrashing
in the underbrush, creatures
flashing in the sea.

                    IV

                    Ten years
ago . . . we have, through strength
and through weakness, through love
and indifference, unerringly come
to this time when we no longer
need—
            at least so we say—
the emulous lovers of old,
the gilded company of kings
and queens, the gold-gross bull,
the snow-fierce, arrowy swan.

The determinate music moves us,
will we or not. Sleeping, awake,
it moves us. We are what we are—
not as we would be or once were—
satisfied. At least so we say.

We have now seen the dead
several times, wrested some pity;
we have come abed like two wooded
children, lost, afraid and yet
trusting,
            wrapt in the sodden
dark, the war and the city-blind
wilderness of windy snow, lost
and yet trusting.

V

        Let us not
lose ourselves in personal pity,
in private awe. The marks of travel
on us, still some haven there has
been, some truth and some joy
in our journey.
                But loved ones,
time's chimerae sucking them into
what shape they will, melt as dawn
before the black wind.
                        Another time
believed? An age more golden
when man could move? That harmony
is broken. The charm flutters
and smokes. Disbelief reverberates
through the hollowness

VI

                of all space
and time to be confirmed. Let us
not lose ourselves in self-pity.
We have come a long way.

Let circumstance rebuke us;
let emptiness puff up a power
the ram and leopard stamp,
bedded ram and raven of our sins;
and then let evil like an alien
cry over us, mirroring its fixed
and aimless fate.
                (These people,
these places, that should compose
a legend where truth is met,
where solemnity would know itself
for all the rest performing it,

storm like foreign tongues,
flickers of the dark.)
                         You,
bending—a recognition—to me,
light the hollow, as another woman
led another man to their resource.

In our embrace what comprehension?
Love, the rest depend upon this union
that estrangement by its strength
approves the worth of, and the force.

The Giant Yea

. . . who can bear the idea of Eternal Recurrence?

I

Even as you went over, Nietzsche,
in your last letter, as ever, you tried
to reach him:
              "Dear Herr Professor,
When it comes to it I too would very much
prefer a professorial chair in Basel
to being God; but I did not dare to go
so far in my private egoism as to refrain
for its sake from the creation of the world."

The past before him, the hateful present
stifling no end of futures with noisy smoke,
what could the Dear Herr Professor, magnificently
sober Jacob Burckhardt, do; how thrust
pitiful hands into what proclaimed itself
a sacred solitude?
                   Maybe too at times,
syringa blowing through his classroom—gape-
mouthed angels Paracelsus pressed into his lectures
in this very room, throwing all Basel

into an uproar and a hatred that finally
drove him out,
                    and familiars like a rout
of mornings bickering to swell the retinue
of Dr. Faustus after breakfast—trumpeting
through the profundity of his pauses,

maybe he could let them, having nothing
to lose in being, be themselves, especially
as there sprang among them heroes out of Raphael
with everything to gain.
                    Even now Astorre
the horseman, in the twinkle of that scholar
eye, spurs quarrying the dark, falcon-plumed,
plunges, a warrior of Heaven, to the rescue
of the youth, fallen with copious wounds,
by this aid exalted.

II

                    Alas, for all the gallant's
audacious charging down the margin of the page,
the Professor's age, parading with its Sunday
family-walks and the thundrous drummers of Basel
in trim, upholstered parks, benumbed him.

What was there for him to do who saw
his begetters, fighting men, furious, mighty
in their pride, come tumbling to such end?

That beauty being slain on the high places
in the midst of its noblest battle, should he,
exclaiming, dare to tell it, publish it
in the streets so prim and polished, to see
the daughters of the philistines rejoice?

He let you go, best emparadised,
or so you said, in the sparkling shadow

of a sword, retiring into frozen heights,
a terrible loneliness, enhanced by sun.

III

At the end, rocks breaking their doors for you,
out poured the shaggy men, hordes of flame
and drunkenness. Solitude, dressed in winds
and falcons, rang, a honeycomb of hailing
voices:
        dancer David; Agamemnon, amethyst
with proud and deadly twisting; Dr. Faustus;
Borgia and Astorre, those human hours,
sowing splendors with their wily wrists.

The peaks, much moved, conscious of the love
that guides by the same capricious path as stars
the agony, the maggot's tooth, hurtling
to your beloved town, stormed its arcades
past the drowsiest beds. God was dead,
long live the gods.
            In that third-floor room,
still going about in your academic jacket
and down at heel, all the heavens rejoicing,
laughing, lifting up your legs,
into the middle of the rout you leaped,
a satyr's dance, as always, the conclusion
of the tragic truth . . .

IV

        You in what we are,
alas, and by your effort that had to fail
have reached us.
        And we go, perhaps as the Herr
Professor did, saddened that we cannot
give ourselves,

the Greeks at last, Paul,
St. Augustine, Luther, Calvin too, surpassed
by the resolution—not time could tame it,
not the mob's indifference—of your fury.

A Working Day

After such a day, too cluttered
for clearing and no way out, no way
to grasp this nameless yet pervasive woe,
after such a day turn to *Genesis:*

ponder the sea before the waves began,
ponder bdellium and the onyx stone
(gold of that land is good), the beasts
got of man's solitude, till woman,
aspiration of his breast, is made. One
flesh, time loitering there.
                    Then "Cursed
is the ground for thy sake." The taste
of the brow's sweat mixed with stubborn
bread this Book knows too well,
the fidgets in ourselves
luxuriate, deft creatures of despair.

Not even the flaming cherubim
could hold that garden in, the snaky weeds
and cankers, plotting and complotting,
avid for this their holiday.

I

You thought,
Thoreau, to sit it out while your giddy
trivial Nineteenth Century preened itself
to death.
For a time, like a halcyon
perched on a spray, and only a few steps
between you and Concord, you settled in Walden—
long as the season of need prevailed;
your land's lord, you sat it out,
secure the valors you had seen, flight
of the seasons, daily in their several lights
remitting more clearly your singular truth.

Then, bold saunterer of morning, gaze fixed
forever on a fresher, greener time, back again,
more private than before.

II

We, in a wood,
dark, myriad, just outside your field,
admit by the radiance of what you discovered
there, the order of beans in a row,
the sweetness of your clearing, the blight
of this we wished for: piper, pigweed,
Roman wormwood?
No name can cast a slowing
spell upon that ragtag army, backed
as much as we by sun and rain. We run
through our assets, friends and events,
the whole summer store.
No one, no thing
can help us. Least of all those who suffered,
tried grief and terror to what seemed their end.
We think, incredulously, of our first glossy
learning, our pride: not one of the past,

the great we assumed we could lean on
forever, has a word for this.

The day, slowly, like a blind idiot
picking in a rock-pit he thinks garden,
passes us by.

III

But you, Henry,
sitting there, going your own way, free
in a world of your own choosing, verge
like that vigorous bean crop between wild
and cultivated fields, were you out of it?

Those companions, mind and body, the populated
self you turned to, unctuous creatures bent
on their own careers, were they to be trusted
any more than the rest?
The rift
that should have made us whole, imperfect
from the start, multiplied first loneliness.
One flesh. At the end, foundering in the blood,
you sat it out, watching the inroads
of the darkening wood.

The Shield

He whose cry enrolled the sea-
shored heavens that, cowed on their crest,
the gods shuddered for the shadows passing,
what would have happened had he lived?

The years passed by, like Asiatics
and Greek Kings conspiring, must steal
this rage which outraged storms and fired
rivers, this gentleness, so gallant the sea
crouched in meditative tears beside him,
even as he strummed,
                the lyre bent
back from war, brimming his heart through
his mortal hands with heroes' undying fame.

That voice at sighing then, only the shield
would stand, defiant, daylight sensible
in its scenes; their feet, whirling
noon- and night-bound fields, sky buckled
by Orion and the interwoven wars, beat
out return:
              sea first, surrounding all,
mountains fleetest through the fog, flashing
for the lightnings there, ridges—cloud

and fire—wrung into the ridges of the sea,
with the great ox's blood commingling.

What he thought he once compelled
now in his receding rises: flood of murdered
eyes, tide of breathless mouths, earth
for air.
      Only the shield would stand,
heavier, day by day, as though the days
massed there, Myrmidon, to mock, the shield
become bedrock of the world.

The Generations

(An old woman is working in her garden.)

      Bent in the sun,
the long burrowing light on my back. Sixty
summers, thirty Augusts here, all borne
in this day. Look out far as the eye can see,
plain the triumph of the shadowless sun.
And John come to this point again between
seared corn and squash, their rows, wave after wave,
gone over him. Bend to the light, my hands
tending and tending.
      Once it was things to be
righted; the dawn brightening in our gaze,
in its clear-eyed light grapes for propping,
creeping vines between our hands, no honey-
bee's labor deep in noon more sweet.
        Late noon,
end of the garden John stands, looking out,
grey boy, to his dim grey youth, faded
denim blending with sky. Come to the kitchen
smelling of earth, mixed with lingering warmth,
arms full of the fruits of our toil, the good
we wrest from the earth.
      Mr. Eckles, nodding,
passes; Reverend Hout pauses: always

the same text—crops and children, changing
weather. Long days spinning from these veins,
out into bleached stacks of noon, to twilight's
quilt-crazed colors, tightened into knots.

Still at night, the body laid away,
once again the mind is free and upright,
swift inside the Good Book's evergreen leaves,
serene for breathing lovely Christian names
of the first fragrance—Ruth alone in the fields,
the Child joyous in His mother's arms.
The words, strangely humming seeds, brought
by wing and beak from farthest lands to nest in,
swell the mind into an heavenly harvest.

Those words we first read, good, open, falling
away . . . in his father's field as we stood,
earth seemed to look to one sure light. Night
it was, but only night for moonlight, turned
as though to look to us. As I to him . . .

that light a burning dark, the laboring breath:
the face—not his, not mine—to be endured
for saving of souls, the making of men, the fiery
face bent over me. Patience, John says.

There he stands, still as any juniper
that crows might use him for their easy perch.
Shrugs, then smiles after the rugged wings,
crackling out, blue-black, as dark's thievish work
inside the light. Looks at me, pale eyes
still flickering with flight, then looks away.

And yet content to stay forever in that
other world; content to dwell in their air,
his father and his father's father beside him,
so he thought; to sit by their window

the whole evening through, their rocker creaking
back and forth in the cracked boards. Content
to keep our boys there.
                        Here in the town, alone
in this rocky garden, I prevailed. And he
said nothing, not after his long working day.
Keeps to the rocker, book sprawled on the floor,
rocks till the needle beaks inside my flesh.
But how the boys respond. Clothes I make over:
John to Joseph; to William; to Edward; back
to John.
                Slow afternoons, the young voices
floating out, eyes caught in the needle's track,
I look up to the cries, my boys all noise
and racing. Like wild things they play. The bodies,
rising, hurl against themselves, playthings
in their game, then snarled in the failing light,
spin with the Eckles children and the Kulps
to the dark till each—behind doubled bush
and wall and tree—is only a dwindled sound.
I pull, cry out, summon them, hanging back, home.

The lessons still to be taught, the boys growing
like fields run wild, tending wherever sun
and wind may blow, whims of the seasons.

He let it go, and I alone to set it right?
No place of mine escapes, not while a bit
of strength sticks to these bones, bent in the sun,
hands in the dirt, sweat glistening like luxury
in the dirt.
                My boys, all noise and racing!
Joseph, frail, twisted by every wind,
and William, growing too fast, grasping—Will-
o'-the-wisp he is—the slenderest thistle-light.

Yet there was Edward, he at least strained up
to greet me as I bent. Roots he gripped,

the first bud, certain summer's whole procession—
ripening through his hand—could be dragged in.
My tenacity, John said. My will indeed:
to know, to do, to hold.
                                    Read to him,
his face among the pictures—the animals gentle
in their alphabet—like something princely
blossomed there, naming after me
with first clear breath flowers, birds, and beasts.
Day by day his mind more avid, lighting
up whatever feeds and brightens it,
the Sabbath like the morning in a dazzling
river picks its promise from his voice.
The sons of Mrs. Eckles and the rest
poor copies beside him, the Church's speaking word,
his brothers in his splendor splendid too.

Will-o'-the-wisp pride is to light us by.
Once angels flew round men, in their wreathings
hymns, jubilations, to honor them. Such heaven
I thought to bend into my house. This earth
that should compose His word nestling us,
one round of seedtime, harvest, trees and hills
resounding, He Himself came down to walk in
and to hear, still mouth it is, all mouth
that—soft as moth and wren, the petalled rose,
the night in steady whispering—gnaws me.

Down in the dark, down in the dust like Him
Who gave up all for us. Most given over,
as my garden, alone out here with the shiftless,
makeshift scarecrow. Not I given over.
The trowel, bone-fast to the hand, strikes
again and again. What plant my heavenly Father
has not planted will be rooted up.

But when? Hack away, with each blow
sweat turns to silvery coilings that, sprouting

fiendish numbers, eat themselves fat in my sweet-
smelling fruits.
               Even as I work who gloats
behind me but these weeds, my sons going,
slips of my will, who but the devil gloating
through these shoots, my sons, their petty thefts,
deceits, his glossy leaves, and whorish books
wherein his good luck lies.
                      And Edward most.
The endless smut he sneaks into his room,
bird and beast and every creeping thing,
like toad-bunched idols at their hideous
delights, befoul the altar, my scoured vessels.
The sacred gift of God, His breath, our lovely
words, forced to couple with the serpent's
hissing blasphemies, their black spawn flaunt
upon a public page.
               Good books, he says,
our age's greatest, as in the Gospels heaven
singing in them, the Maker's world. Compare
such with God's chosen! What the purpose,
where the promised end?
                Silken words
to set off filth of lies, these slugs, a slime
across the shiny leaf, coiled round and round
each other, one writhing brown obscenity.

Rip them out and rip though some good go.

And Edward there—sheets crumpled in my hands—
O let me not think of it—to see the face
of that fury in him, flaring,
as he flares behind him in the doorway
John and all the gloating weeds I thought
I plucked, rows of them, wave after wave
going over them, the Garden—leaves just before
their fall—crackling flames.

                              Only such slugs
can cross this rift? Pull down and stamp, they speed,
devouring, through the fields.
                              This ravage Eve
first birthed, Satan, spreading plague, the slugs
pitching far-flung tents even as they
turn the world to dust. They are what they
were meant to be, faithful their brief hour
to their given task.
                      And Edward no less faithful,
already begun the life-long desert journey,

myself striding, monstrous, in his meanest
deeds! I reach out . . . he that is without sin . . .
not even him, the late chance, the last hope,
gone, gone out of my hands . . .
                              my father rejected,
the first Father, and my youngest, father
of my future . . . are they to be merely
unfolding, thriving of my wretchedness—
my sons, my sins!
                  Flesh knows a will of its own—
weed. My will beyond my will, how much
can two hands do? Patience. The patience forever
demands. The husbandman waits for the precious fruit,
and has long patience for it, until he knows
the early rain and the latter.
                              But when the rains
fall so fast, so full, wilderness alone
prevails? Must we feel our way back all
the way of thorn and rot to glimpse the anger
of the flaming angel, else we push
God out of us, God altogether?
                              This separateness.
It stretches through words, chores, my mocking steps.
Clutch as I may, will nothing bend to me?

Lilies lolled on the breeze, the lordly hollyhocks,
more glorious than Solomon, they toil not,
neither do they spin—like him out there,
flushing the light. Nor the gnats, a gossamer,
heating in shameless lust the last of the sun.

Light failing at last, for all that I do,
down on all fours in this crowded bed, worm
and the dark, conspiring, leer at my back
(Eckles, Mrs. Eckles, oily Hout),
the glittering, unregenerate stars.
                              Look up,
old tattered scarecrow. Sky is earth, these weeds
white sides, tarnished, of a truth unending,
of men past ruth and time.
                              Patience? Forgive?
Blow, hack and pull that a clearing be made.
Pluck the weed out, pluck now, or let flesh go.
Else why a soil with hands, a will of its own,
if it must yield.

The Fire at Alexandria

Imagine it, a Sophocles complete,
the lost epic of Homer, including no doubt
his notes, his journals, and his observations
on blindness. But what occupies me most,
with the greatest hurt of grandeur, are those
magnificent authors, kept in scholarly rows,
whose names we have no passing record of:
scrolls unrolling Aphrodite like Cleopatra
bundled in a rug, the spoils of love.

Crated masterpieces on the wharf,
and never opened, somehow started first.
And then, as though by imitation, the library
took. One book seemed to inspire another,
to remind it of the flame enclosed
within its papyrus like a drowsy torch.
The fire, roused perhaps by what it read,
its reedy song, raged Dionysian, a band
of Corybantes, down the halls now headlong.

The scribes, despite the volumes wept
unable to douse the witty conflagration—
spicy too as Sappho, coiling, melted
with her girls: the Nile no less, reflecting,
burned—saw splendor fled, a day consummate

in twilit ardencies. Troy at its climax
(towers finally topless) could not have been
more awesome, not though the aromatic house
of Priam mortised the passionate moment.

Now whenever I look into a flame,
I try to catch a single countenance:
Cleopatra, winking out from every joint;
Tiresias eye to eye; a magnitude, long lost,
restored to the sky and the stars he once
struck unsuspected parts of into words.
Fire, and I see them resurrected,
madly crackling perfect birds, the world
lit up as by a golden school, the flashings
of the fathoms of set eyes.

A Trip Through Yucatan

You have, in a sense,
been through it all; each experience
has known you, like a Swiss clock
in the middle of the room, forcing
all things to its rickety breathing.

Abruptly then the one out
that you see—rather than swinging
in and out, forever, on a crazy
and precarious stick, pretending
to be another hour, another place,

one of you for one time, another
for the next, and never meeting—
the one out is a break-down.
Then all things can, with a sigh,
forget you . . .
                yet after days
of snow, too swiftly falling to be
accounted for, in the middle of it
a moon appears, absurdly beautiful
and warm . . .
                like the dinner-
party you have just come from where
the speaker assured you your French

accent reminded him of his trip
through Yucatan:
                 a group
of Americans, a few Spaniards,
and several French, all insisting
they understood each other's speech;
only he, interpreting, knew the truth.

    Madly, the epitome of tact,
he hopped about from one to the next,
trying to keep their ignorances
from them . . . I have stopped jumping;
and moon-wise, in a sense, arises

    that last implacable light-
heartedness, like emerging mid-jungle
into a jubilant calm, a clearing
of florid birds and plumaged flowers
that set the feastday of the storm.

House of Fire

I

To burn is surely bad, to be
possessed by greed or lust or anger . . .

Down the pathway pebbles clatter
into brush more ashen than the rocks
that mount the cliff; beyond it windows,
flaring, flood the light through vines,
entangled with the thudding wind,
as litter, crackled underfoot, puffs
up the dust of countless little deaths.

And yet in the abandoned field
below, through this intense decaying
and its acrid breath, a freshness wells
as if an April, some forgotten day of,
starting up out of the time's debris,
looked round amazedly.

II

The man
Job squats among the soot and ashes,
his complaints mingling with the smoke.

He sifts with peeling fingers cinders
of that once his boundless joy:

sheep, camels, oxen and she-asses;
seven sons, three comely daughters,
the tender dewy branch unceasing who
guaranteed the generations of his name
as of his various unique features;
and his fame gone through the streets
a bounteous morning to proclaim him—

    these sift, soft flakes, breaking
      in the flurry of his cries.

III

Yet what lust or greed or anger,
what burning in this house of fire
beyond what becomes a man, that man
who girt up his loins according
to the Lord's command?
                And sifting
flakes, he strews them in a drunkenness
of despair about his head, the last
fruits of his efforts, the folly
of all living.
          Surrender all,
the Whirlwind says, whatever endeared
you even as it made Me dear to you.

No less lovely than the first arriving
leaves at falling; through the nakedness
the mighty music, unmitigated, enters.

Dew all night an ice upon the branch,
the cedars cleaving in the wind,
like a huge flock gathering

in the boughs, each tree achieves
its height the moment when it crashes.

IV

And yet that leveling Wind
did He not summon as witnesses
His freckled, much-loved creatures,
numberless as leaves, yet loved
for individual, self-willed features?

Mane flamboyant, hoof and nostril
bristlings of the mine of fire,
the horse that, leaping forth, saith "Aha!"
no less to battle than to pelting hail;
Leviathan grown tender, weltering
out his rage, the boiling ocean docile
in waves self-absorbed—
                    these, springing
like the hurricane, soft cooing words
around His lips, from God's own fingertips,
warm with them He warms, exult Him surely
in the grandeur and unique particulars
of their pride.

V

                Sky and earth
are held in a twilight's rushing
furious fire, earth and sky the route
of pawing hoofs, till all the colors drain
into one conflagration.
                    But here
as I pause on the little wooden bridge,
the waters, shielded by two arching pines,
needles heaped below, purl into a cat's paw.

Coolly the ripples from one side,
pursuing their dappled course, are crossed
like a shuttle by ripples from the other
till they pour together—yet still
themselves—in the next step
of their streaming.

VI

And so the sea
is fed, and so the fire, the rampant waves
and flames flared up in stubborn homage
to their fathering first desire.

The Medium

1965

The Medium

Fog puffed from crusted snow, rain sputters
midnight over them. Her words, a kind
of browsing in themselves, rise, cloud-bound,
by him in the bed.
              She says, "I know
now why I have no memory. It's come to me,
a revelation. I must keep my thinking
open; I am not, like others, scribbled
all over by whatever happens."
                      He answers,
"Revelation? That's what you've always been
to me; by way of you have I not slithered
under the skin of things?"
                  "Cleansed of words,
my fears and doubts cast off, the fears
that words invent, I see each thing, free
at last to its own nature, see it free
to say exactly what it is."
                "As for our primo-
genitor," he chimes in, "beside his twilit doorway, bent after the long day's chores
on the seraphic visit, meantime calling
things by their first name again."
                  "You won't
believe that people waken in my sleep
and like the moon, self-enlightened, speak

a language I don't know, move in a language
so itself one needn't know."
                              "Dreams,"
he nods, "do such things, like you attune
the dim as well as the emphatic phrases
I live in, the world become a bob-
bingly translucent globe, that round,
piped like Aeolus' impassioned winds
into a tiny bag,
                    then popped, grape-
sweet, upon my tongue, for you beside me
sounding its fanfare. Such cornucopia
your lip and hand."
                      "How you do go on!
Unless you curb these peacock speeches you
love strutting in, how will you ever hear
another's words?
                    Now listen to me. My father
lives again, in the special space I keep
for him here in my sleep, as he really is,
nothing but his fundamental voice,
directness daylight always must obscure,
cluttered as we are with long dead habits
and with failures, rage, my own and his,
encrusting us."
                  The dream flushed on her still
addresses him through her without a sound:
"The time will come when your time comes;
the role meant for you slamming shut,
none of your wit, your artful dodgings,
able to hide you then, each thing you do
at last will prove effective, like a lion
grinding through your side."
                              As moonlight
brims the fog, he hears, in books lined up
around them, richly scored, a honey pouring
through the words, the language passing
speakers, too imperious for words.

In the Round

Catching yourself, hands lathery
and face ajar, inside the glass,
you wryly smile; watching, you know
you're in for it:
               and in the twinkle
of your eye the horny butting goat
and jutting horny bull, the weasel,
goose bedraggled and the wren
with greedy bill go flashing by;
there too, recoiled as from the shadow
of itself in a teetering pool, claws
contracted to one cry, the spider
crouches in its den.
                  What gusto
can it be that blows its violence
through a locust's violin, mad summer
burnishing in such midge mouths?

These the routine heroes, poised,
in resolution black as bulls,
deadlocked in a din of warriors
grappling centaurs—prizes near:
a heifer nibbling grass; the rouged
and gossamer girl, nothing diaphanous
as the fearful hope that flits,

a fire's touch, inside her breath,
each prize forgotten—on a vase.

One wonders how the clay withstands
not only time, but what such hands,
great hearts, command from one another,
art and earth, the audience amazed.
Still, though clay crack, necks
break, twitchy as a cock, they stand,
engrossed and going on, a Bach
of a beetle, strutting like a yokel,
nightlong at its tongs and bones.

White Elephants

. . . and were these in the ark as well?

Alone except for one bowlegged, bounding
cur whose yipping scored the frozen world,
that afternoon we tracked the neighbor grounds,
two people and a dog in a sprawled estate.

The snow before and after, trees black above
it as below, had molded to the dips
and curvings of the ground. Winds too like drifts
folded round the stubble sticking through.
Beyond, the Catskills, blue under blue-honed sky,
humped, recumbent days on days forsaken.

Following the road-bend to the coach-house,
we sidled through its doors; there considered
its first inhabitants—their shiny flanks
and tails, their whinnyings and oaten smells—
could they be seen in oaken panelings,
hoofs clattering still upon the stony floor.

Out of it, we skirted the dirty mansion,
these several years fitfully alive, lurched
to one side for the weather's shifty weight,

its corniced cherubim and cedars, carved
in cedar, mostly shed.
                    The formal gardens
at their stiffest now, their fountain billowed,
snowbird struggling in its ice-jagged flight,
the Hudson just below had banked, a moonlight,
freezing while it fell, one rigor mortis.

As if fearing those the storm must satisfy
(the stone-pale woman in the alcove, arms
set round two children, and a dog beside,
caught in his friskiness as in their spell),
we went no nearer.
                    But winds struck us, fluster
at the pane of flakes off rubbing boughs.
Or was it blur of frantic beckonings,
now less than thistledown upon the blast,
a curtain flickering the moonlit-shoulder-
shadowed waltzes, glimpses of the Danube,
as from a time that closed with the passing
of the last great lady of the house?

It never closed:
                    cracks pried by children
and damp cellar kin, relentless for their chance,
the house shook, shook out its occupants
to quake again with merriment of those
for the first time enjoying total tenancy.

And O what marrying was there, what free-
for-all in mirror, spider, paired-off drapes;
the letters, scattered in a corner, wound up
with ants and wasps at capers, fern's sly mind.

The seed in itself after its own kind,
in each smuggled the deeds (stowed away
below as in the rafters' crevices

dragons, bats, pigweed) that grew the Garden
beyond itself, flowered above the Flood:

crimes, failures, flowering too, the first root
must have journeyed through to this, the cluster
it would become for not a few to carry,
smoky over purple as of some shy episode,
a rainbow tangled glistening in its foliage.

And still the rickety mansion stood; the little
dog, yipping round and round, snuffling out
huge tracks, lolloped over its racy, curving lawns
till the mountains swayed, a graceful, lurching,
trunk-entwining, cloud-behowdahed two by two.

The outgrounds rallying, the stallions that
once galloped here, cows nodding to their stalls,
the bugs and mice tucked in their cranny darks
like jewels gleaming in a mummied tomb,
all seemed to fly to a single joyous yoke.

And clouds for twilight flushed with riches.
Days on days swept in a rush, at once
the dirty snow went bright, those first tracks up
and down the dips and curvings of the air,
brown shoots off like till-now-drowsing crows,
the flake-doves off, no rest for their feet
beyond the stubble waking in their beaks.

A World to Do

for Jeffrey

"I busy too," the little boy
said, lost in his book
about a little boy, lost
in his book, with nothing

but a purple crayon
and his wits to get him out.
"Nobody can sit with me,
I have no room.
     I busy
too. So don't do any noise.
We don't want any noise
right now."
     He leafs
through once, leafs twice;
the pictures, mixed with windy
sighs, grow dizzy,
       world
as difficult, high-drifting
as the two-day snow that can
not stop.
     How will the bushes,
sinking deeper and deeper,

trees and birds, wrapt
up, ever pop
              out again?
Any minute now the blizzard,
scared and wild, the animals
lost in it—O the fur,

the red-eyed claws, crying
for their home—may burst
into the room. Try words
he's almost learned

              on them?
He sighs, "I need a man here;
I can't do all this work
alone."

      And still, as though
intent on reading its own
argument, winter continues
thumbing through itself.

The Reapings

Firstlings of grief,
pain in all its sweetest fat
and dew, abounding in my sinews
its sinews, like a mettlesome, gay
youth . . .
                    years later,
the fields gone over a thousand
times, every flower spied on,
every weed, like a royal being,
golden foreigner,
                    as though
one, not seeing, might forget,
let loose its secret, the reality . . .
years later, the basic truths,
their seasons
                    in each season,
gone over and over, still grief
strikes, a new-forged arrow, finds
out fresh wounds, its resource,
surprising, relevant,
                    of pain.
The hands clutch themselves
in the wrestle; how learn
to let go like a nakedness in this

fluent fall,
                a warbling rain?
And how be thankful, name
with love this one that seeks
me out, demands a stature of me,
a strength,
                so arrogant for me,
I hardly knew I own? Breaking,
I lie there, threshed, before me,
gifts, the firstlings, weathered
on that flying stone.

As I Forget

for David Schubert (1913–1946)

I rummaged for that thought again,
that feeling and that image where,
as it burst forth, my life began.

The dead, I said, whatever we do,
alone can tell us that we have
to learn: precisely as they owe

what life they now enjoy to us,
in turning to them we must grow
the more alive and thereby blessed,

their wisdom gathering on us. Sure
of it, I tried to struggle back.
But fighting every clever pleasure

of forgetting hemmed the way,
I soon despaired of meeting him
who might have told me, passing day,

how to withstand these temptings and
deceits by how much he had paid.
I soon despaired, my groping hand

huge with emptiness. And then
I said, Is only loss, its strength
ransacking all, one steady dun,

the thing I have to learn, and there
that image, feeling, thought embraces
me with grave and finished air?

Though pansies, lionhearted scholars,
ponder sorrow, in his words,
they utter gaiety and splendor.

Of blooms a girl the mignonette
engrossing me, I have him, am him,
and most of all, as I forget.

The Moral

The dark figures, lunged ahead,
out of their twisted lust for heaven
and the stars, into the sea, into the dirt,
your father, mine, and that benighted
company,
         aeries predatory birds
grow sleek in, their lives crackling
like holocausts, the concentration camps
where tortures, working out hell's
ideology, excel,
           those, sounding
through our minds like bells, ringing us
into the catacombs that man can be,
shall they also light us, lead
us through the midnight
              of our days?
We have warmed our hands at many strange
fires, many stray. The summer's jew's-
harp has twanged out hot blues
of some superior pain,
            its fireflies
faraway torches for a pilgrimage
to altars crammed with sacrifices. Cries,
backs bent, glistening in bloody sweat,

to accurate, gay lashes,
                    the shriek,
a phosphorescence sizzling, of the mouse,
accomplished in the likely clutches
of the hawk, like lilies in a paradigm
spell out the moral
                    of our tale.
Whatever has happened, diverse ravishings
that love to bask in balmy weather
of a scream, the passionate failures,
the perfect despairs, these never fail us.

Into Summer

Some days ago, to stop the leaping
weeds, on both sides of the path
workmen scorched these fields.
A short time after, as he passed
the charcoal-velvety, zigzag tracks,
he smelt the strange blend of the
burnt and the growing.
                              But now,
just over the black, something flags,
green flicked here and there,
but mostly a transparent papery
brown, like stubborn ghosts caught
in the fire and yet come through,
nodding as though to say, "This is
as much as we can do."
                              And he who
tried to pierce the classroom tedium,
to move his students to a grove,
a clearing where the green remains,
recalls some struggled into words,
then fallen back, eyes flickering
a second as though caught with sun.

And they, like one's best hopes
and feelings, singed yet wrangling

through, knowing nothing but the need
to go on, into summer?
                          Soon,
of their own greed and by the tangle
of numbers, the weeds will do
what the greasy fire was meant to.

But now each must heed the music
mumbling in him—in some crazy way,
on top of the brown, green sticks out,
and a whitish, tiny kind of flower—
that strange blend of the burnt
and the growing.

Through the Strings

I

To be free of the fingers,
the need to be making,
to be slaking the moon
under the tongue:
> to be free
of the feelings that weave,
siren, savage, adder-like
striking, through the lyre.

Again and again, gasped
in the seethe of its leaves,
August requires breath;
November, strident, chafes
at my tuning.
> Let rains—
the lightnings nestled
by their coil—ride, cradled
in clouds; let winds, tree-
modulated, nod.

II

> But now
the lightfoot season, slid

through metal and the lidded
seed,
     my lyre like dead wood
taken, greedily confronts
with the stare of the thing
called five petals.

III

     To be free
of the fingers—why should she,
gone, except as she cries out
in me, seeking some body, be
a wedding of winter and summer
so singly?
     Through the rock-
ribbed earth she draws me,
gentian, twilit here, elsewhere
for the somber lights passed
through—
     the fingers once
love- and passion-clever, moans
dirt-stuffed, with glances sealed
into the root—
          guttering smoky,
cloven faces . . .
       so singly
as though the flower of the long
tongue in fruition's final outrage
uttered the one unerring word.

IV

Long and long I have stormed
through the strings, the wrangle
under the breath, the Dog toothing
ravenous heads in the groin.

She gone at the turning,
the others, charmed, let loose,

ensnarled in my song, stay with me,
clamoring for more.
                    Too long
I lie, too long in this slow river-
bed the leaves make, huddled
dead sighs.

                    V

            Last smiting of strings

(shades, responsive again—
                    dense
verdure, risen undertow, of listening
cypresses, apt pitch-pines, river-
rapt willows—
                    my loyal convoy,
a match for the dark, shall I not
bring her back?):
                    bunched notes
plucked, petal by petal, a resonant
curve throbs through my fingers:

leaped above the sprung bar,
gaze, and gazing breast, thigh
glistening:
                    one tentative step, tripped
falling, fallen, far beyond that
viper spite, her disappearing
surpasses my speediest cry;
                    but there,
there, in that white a loitering . . .

                    VI

try catching it, no watery moonlight
more elusive.
                    The motes have gone
out, like echoes, the notes, of a cry—
mine? hers?—in mockery.

And nothing
more than racketing chats, flicker
like eyelids of sparrows, low
to the ground, oaks also forsaking,
poplars in droves?

VII

Fingers, writhing,
fang themselves; the feelings trample,
mountainous. How bear such pitch
of yearning,
this strange hand
upon the lyre, strums by mine, strums
through, now strums—a storm begins
to stir in me—alone?
Grown, grown
with every breath, the notes backfire,
buffet heart. (This covey after her,
did that twanging bring them?)
Drop
me, lyre, drop. And play as you will
in spiders' tautened nets, the aspens
saying you, unfettered winds.
Play
through the women, fury-bitten,
dammed by me. Let them, cries brimmed
to howls, attack.
Like the gentian
under this rock, flying me free,
sticks, clods, deft hands at me, I am
plucked.

VIII

Surely I rejoin her
whose love brought harmony
I did not need to play,

brought peace
    past savage night,
highnoon, a sweet extinction
of all fear, all longing,
till all loss began.
    Extinction
now must grant me peace again,
her face above, so fitting
then I thought it
    my own
doing only, birds too, flowers,
out of singing, summer-breed-
ing tunes.

    IX

    Breath quicker than wind,
I glide through the arching gate
of their stones,
    down the route
ripped petals make upon the spurting
stream, into the grass, ground
opening.
    That one word going
under, earth's tide, the white
flower—
    see! the round sigh
of her (torches splutter behind,
the cloven faces), hand's last wave,
sky clutched in her hand—
       surges
over, filling the mouth . . .

    X

    he, never
again looking past that shoulder,
reins in the hands of a will
that brooks no consent.

On Stuffing a Goose

(after overhearing some students talk
   knowingly of D. H. Lawrence)

Is this fame then and what it is to be
really alive, to go on living after flesh,
having failed, has been officially
hauled away?
                 To cast a moment's spell
upon some distant man and girl, a feeling
of familiarity in a gust of fragrance
in a summer's night,
                        of loneliness
made roomier as they recall his anguish,
as though flesh alone, one time and place,
one wife, a single set
                        of friends
were too confining and that life must be
let out to mine its basic cadence finally
in our pondering of it,
                        free of any
obligation save the pleasure that we take
in it. . . . My father was a great hand
at stuffing geese.
                 In the cellar dark
he'd keep one penned. Knees grappling it,

he'd ram a special mash with dippers
of water down its throat.
                              In time
that crate began to bulge; past waddling,
goose managed only belchy squawks.
We knew it ready.
                              Somewhere in all this
I have a sense of what it is to be really
alive. Somewhere in the celebration
of that goose,
                       throned on a shiny
platter, for its mellow crackling skin
a jovial martyr, piping savors of a life
well lived,
                       our heart's gladness
in the occasion of picking the juicy meat
from the sides and the bones, in that
and remembering the sense abides.

Two for Heinrich Bleucher

A Satyr's Hide

I

In smoky light the students gawk
at pluming, reeled off from their lips,
as the speaker, groping, breaks
through words into some other air.

But one, apart, till now squinting
through the fumes he tries to fan
with a heavy lilac cluster, jeers:
"I am not difficult enough, not
like these by apathy alluring him.

He thinks persuasion can convert
them into peers, their dust at last
alive as though, stirred, the gods
were laboring within.
                  And see
the grown-up men he hobnobs with,
artists fuddled as their paints,
perverts, crackpots, moldy peddlers
of ideas.
             Nobility gleaned from swamps!"

II

To see the divine matters, the stars that,
foiled by some events and fouled by others—
wars and trials and deaths—serenely shine ...

one, old, bald, mottled, with a flattened beak,
bulbous as a growth under a toadstool,
in dress a bumpkin, barefoot in some kind
of fit ("not the sign of contemplation?"),
and in the middle of battle, onelegged, day-
long standing like a crane.
                            Or, chortling away,
joining ragged kids at hopscotch ("who's
to say wisdom itself, shirt bunched round
its spindly shanks, was not skipping too");

one with striplings, especially the handsome,
in any wretched tavern, rattling up his heels
the whole night through, relentless, prodding them
("beyond themselves, in chase perhaps of something only glimpsed, driving joy").

And then, cock crowing, nothing more to do
than watch the boats bustling at the wharves,
the bales and slaves ("spices like nodding winds
aroused, with distant names and places puffed
from sails. Athens travel enough: do not
the stars each night arrive, the famous gods,
incognito?").
                            Unfit for public office,
jester, gibing, bitter toward his superiors,
in court and out, with lingo, slops from
gutters still fresh on it, flaying alive.

Spellbinder too, throwing all who care to hear
into confusion and dismay as though
to say their lives are nothing but a slave's

("for the difficulties over which they, failing
to see through, toil, turmoil themselves"),
so making it impossible for some
to go on as they were.
                                        A man to be trusted?
Little more than the lover he played along with,
drunk ("who ever saw him, wine unmixed,
goblet on goblet flashing like his wit,
inebriate?"), in very drunkenness
("of love") proclaiming him a grotesque, Silenus,
preceptor of mad Dionysus.
                                        ("Remember
what those curious figures stowed: musk
like fragrances deep-wooded, weathered leaves
keep, caperings among the fauns and dryads,
deities at their numerous delights.")

That favorite pupil, crowned with violets,
bright ribbons dangling, wayward under splendor
like a fire, sprung full-panoplied
from the master's head and thigh ("full-panoplied,
as he himself admitted, had he heeded
that voice reclaiming him to his best nature
he forever fled"), with other young bloods
launched on matters so divine, might tread
down Athens, shiny pebble in his reeling.

("Might indeed: sealed off as he was,
his beauty dazzling, only havoc fed him,
deadly respite from his golden curse.
But the other without the State, he knew,
and the lovely haven, sovereign polis,
of its language, would be worse than dead.")

The old one—imagine it, death just ahead,
eternity approaching ("a sense of time
for everything")—amused himself by taking
for the first time in his life to verse-making

and the flute: ("a Paean to Apollo")
and fables, appropriately, out of Aesop!

A satyr play ("the true philosophy");
so cast him, judged by some the loftiest crag
in cloud-capped—temples like clouds; roads, markets,
rumbling with beauty—fastidious Athens.

"Never forget he did not have that hide
for nothing; shaggy capering, the goat-dance,
rooted him wherever, the course he followed
on the flute.
        Risk it was no doubt a star
standing out in the open and confidently
twirling about itself, risk or that real thing
sometimes called folly, notes laureling his head;
yet earthiness and the mystery therefrom
never left him a moment:
                  divine matters."

III

The lilac spray, plucked from one
peak of late spring, resilient still
as the words move through it, seems
to tingle in his hand.
          A deep lilac
breath, the speech in it the air
for ancient voices, rising, rousing
coupled shapes, he sees what man
might be,
        man finding out his place
within the frieze, a marble, breathing
heroes, gods, and satyrs, creatures
confident in flight.
         And in the drift
of words he lets the cluster sway,
its top clump heaviest for buds

closest together,
                    still unopened
as though the life in the lilac
had surged through this stem
and on the way, tarrying,
                    burst
into flower, then sped to the top,
but cut off before it could gather,
hung there,
                    nubbly grapes or the plume
of a boy smitten in his first encounter.
Purpler they than the lavender open.
Yet the words soaring, he half expects
these last buds to respond.
                    But death
always more on them, like lids that,
nearly lifted, now certainly would
not, he watches the lilac following
the laws, the scent gradually waning,
the head drooping.
                    And when the speaker
stops, he offers it to him:
"If you will take it; I have had it
this hour."
                    That one, flourishing it,
"The gift, you told me once, depends
on the receiver."
                    On the receiver,
but also on the giver who,
in that delicious hunger of giving,
the last, the loveliest, loftiest love
of all, the light and scent of a self-
rewarding joy—gives with no notion
of reply.

The Wine-Skin Foot

Loose not the wine-skin foot, thou chief of men,
Until to Athens thou art come again.

ORACLE OF DELPHI

. . . a rolling stone . . .

I

The wine-skin foot?
Well as one can he hides it, hid it most
when the land where he first found it
turned into a howling wilderness.

A growing wolf howl, steady twister, blew
through Berlin into Paris. And he saw it—
tyranny, what he loved crushed by the treason
of the state, at last full-blown, bloody—
countless death to stay.
                    (Did not his gentle
friend, to save his son from bestiality and worse, kill him.) Words and deeds
there were, the gods, sacred freedom, dance
and song to smuggle out.
                    The Delphi in him
urging him on, four times over by choice

a fugitive, barefoot through mud and rocks,
the flinty cold of more than half of Europe,
living on wild berries, the fulfillments,
raptures of the hunted:

              in certain seasons
thrilling as ever the pain inside his bones.

Cast on this shore, the language of his youth
much like the rubble of the world he fled
and foreign phrases, stubborn on the tongue
as new terrains to aging sinews, futile
also, once again he tries through speech
the market-place and the arena use
to reach the latest young.

                The magic works:

II

Exchange goes on, a subtle flow-
ing in and out of lilac breath,
exchange a dialog as though
someone were feeding, feeding
were thus fed:

            the well-assorted
voices in his voice that rage
with lilac, grape, the open sea,
as it rolls up, the secrets
of one's life, lovely on its crest:

and morning like that flambeau
grating fury first ignited,
morning flung from crag to crag,
grown lucid in the wrangling wills:

bow-twang and lyre-, speedy passage
to the spires of snow-glimmer-
ing Parnassus and the summits

over it of stars, the dark
a shadow of what avid thought?

and still the light upon his words
as day, plunging, gladly lingers
in the wings of sportive birds,
the lady's owl-eyed, leafy gazing.

III

Wherever you go you will be a polis.

But where is Athens, once that city
in the clouds? Now nameless rubble
most of it, many times nameless—
lilac, asphodel and poppy
famous through its cracks and stubble—

ruins in the wind of what
mad whirling, monstrous with delight,
rushed by, a passion beyond purpose,
hope, too fierce for shape, Athens
pebble shiny in its reeling,

pillars fallen as their gods,
then raised again to fall again
for Vandals, Turks, Venetians, Franks,
the Romans, its own restless will
and a hundred moods of tameless time:

like an enormous cicada shell
of some now-far catastrophe,
the crumbling Parthenon.
                              Strange
that as one stands in it—
                              a dancing
in and out with civil light,
those airy massive girls, that eagle

lit on steadfast wind—
            and gazes
through its broken skeleton
the town below should look so whole,
so radiant.
            And here, the dusk
wine-spilt on the hills, the stars
as they leaned on these pillars once,
near for the centuries ago
they first began, in twinkling airs
repeat their haunting names again.

IV

A pebble in the mouth of one
whose tongue rolls round, a pebble sounding plumbless fathoms, fames of time.

And it rolls round, metropolis
and temples, traffic rumbling beauty,
clouds resounding, tides:
                    the wine-
skin foot, released, leaps forth,
capricious as a satyr, dulcet
drunkenness where, mouth to mouth
gods and men combining,
                    Athens—
rooted as the strophes of the stars
within the wine-sack of the grape,
like dawn swept down on us through leaf
and flake, the lilac's sudden rippling—
purls through lips and shaping hands.

Clothes Maketh the Man

(to be read aloud awkwardly)

How hard it is, we say,
how very hard. Clearly no one can say
these cluttered lines and make them
stride or make them stay. No actress
in the land—the best have tried—
can find a pattern or a rhythm
in such befuddled monologue.
                                        Concede,
I say, it is a role to test the mettle
of a Bernhardt who, wigged, without a leg
and in a ragged voice could—so they say—
strike any rock-like audience to tears,
this with only the alphabet.
                                          Maybe,
you say, maybe. But then the alphabet
by Racine, no less.
                            And I am depressed.
Ah me, I am depressed to think how we,
with many more outspoken words, submit
to mutterings and silence, only answer
fitting our despair.
                            How hard it is,

we say, how very hard, that we should find
ourselves stuck in such muck.
                        Oh well,
I say, maybe when we haven't understood
each other long enough, it will prove
stubborn stuff that we can carve.

Already Goya knew the sharp rebuff
of nakedness. With nothing between
he almost wrung his naked Maja's neck,
as though he'd stuck the head of one girl,
a much beloved, on the body of another
(for less aesthetic uses, say), and they
would not set, not in the daring solvent
of his paints.
                    His Maja draped was
a far different matter. I say! I never
thought I'd prefer a dressed girl to one
undressed. Even for me, I see, it's later
than I guessed.
                    So let's go home to bed,
Renée, and dress and dress and dress.

Studying French

some thirty years too late
(the rhythms do declare themselves,
the glints, through clumsy clouds,
through stiff-as-frozen clods,
the flowers in their revery),

I, who love our English words
and loll in them against
the several terror and the cold
like any little furry animal
grown cocky in his hole, begin

to understand past supple words
the language you and I grope
toward and, reaching, wander in
among the periods of doubt,
those long ice-numbing nights

when deserts seem to travel
us at their own stately speed
and fury like a moony beast,
a speechless, glacier-capable,
goes poking its rough tongue,

so searching, into the crevices,
the weaknesses, of everything.
For one long given over
to another tongue this French
is much too hard. It makes me

doubt myself, my easy hold
on everything, and everything.
I who debonairly strolled
(I rallied them, I twitted them
with double talk) among my words

like one among his animals,
once wild, but now their strength,
their rippling colors, blazoned
on him, can smell once more
the threatening smolder, smoke

behind them, open fields so fine
for pouncings and hot blood,
the void in flower we go out
to meet, hand clutched in hand,
as it ransacks us for its tutoyer.

Ruins for These Times

To hell with holy relics,
sniffing like some mangy dog
after old, dead scents (saints?),
those that went this way before
and went. More shambling about
in abandoned, clammy churches
and I abjure all religion,
even my own!
              It's much too late
to heft a Yorick skull and, ear
to it as to a surf-mad shell,
hold forth foul breath to breath
on man's estate.
              What's more
I, plundered, plundering,
out of these forty odd bumbling
years have heaped up spoils
with spells compelling
enough, my own:
              a father
who keeps coming apart however
I try to patch him together

again. Old age too much for him,
the slowly being picked to pieces
as a boy with a fly, he hopped
a spunky horse and left
change gaping in the dust.
                          Mother
too who would not watch herself
turn into blind and stinking
stone, took things into her own
hands, finished a rotten job
with a rush.

                    II

                    But lest I seem
too personal, let me cite
the grand, efficient, ruin-making
fashion of our time.
                    This earth,
a star, brave and portly once,
now like a chimney belches
filthiest smoke, fallout
of roasting human meat the air
we breathe;
                    the ember-eyes
of millions I have never seen
(yet relatives the more for this,
stand-ins for the role
I missed by sheerest accident)
flare up within my dream's
effective dark.
                    O let Odysseus,
Hamlet, and their sparkling
ilk grope after; here's
a midnight ought to satisfy
the genius in them.

III

                    Let them.
What's the mess of Europe,
late or antique, great or antic,
to the likes of me?
                    Pottering
about in my own cluttered memory,
I turn up, still in full career,
my grandfather, muscles sprung
from dragging packs through miles
of factories:
                    a grandmother
who bore, conscripted lifelong
to the total war of hunger
and a strange new world,
three families on her back
and then outwore them all
as she outwore her ailments,
one enough to fell a warrior:

that friend whose breath shaped
songs desperately debonair
out of our snarling dog-eat-dog
accomplishments.

IV

                    There too
I poke out bits, still standing,
from my wrecks, begun in fervor,
aspiration, joy:
                    those passages
through which the morning strode,
enlightened in its retinue,
choke on the plaster falling,
raspy stenches, refuse of lives
trapped in them.

Is the building
lust for ruin so strong in those gone
before that I and mine are nothing
but a story added, foundation
for new ruins?
                    The prospect
that seemed the way to heaven
glimmers mainly with the promise
of a final storm, a monument
of glittering bones to gratify
most dogged fates.
                    Our own.

An Opening Field

for Stefan Hirsch

To mind and not to mind,
to be exposed, open
(like a barn, its rafters
and its walls collapsing,
and the summer, prying
through the gaps, rolls
round among unbinding mows,
its tumbled light so sifted
in the strawy rifts), to mind
and not to mind,
                    ignoring death,
yet for, awaiting it like one
long played on that the airs
recall his sense of being,
open so that wasps may enter,
throbbing like a central nerve,
wasps and the many moods
the summer, simmering
from one bed as it wakens,
then the next, is given to . . .

you see your painter friend,
once buoyant to the world,

now broken by the flogging
blows his gentleness
exposed him to: through love,
no less than the world's
indifference, these strike.
And as he, dragged along
by his dog on their daily
latenoon walk, draws near,

you ask, "Where are you
going?" At first he fails
to notice you, looks about
as though a voice he cannot
see were calling him. Then,
like one returned from far
away, he peers at you.
"Geh kotzen," he replies.
"But first I've got to find
someone with shiny shoes."

"That's dangerous," you warn.
"Add to the mess already here,
and we'll be over our heads
in it." He nods. Then gazing
up through the cleft
in the trees to the field
beyond: "How fine it is!
No matter what we do
or say, it still goes on
the way it has to, lovely."

The field, light full,
as though the sun delayed,
among the border-sloping
trees and in and out
the solitary trees, has
slowly mellowed, a meeting—
as from its own accumulating—

of mild and generous,
intensely calm (a master's
fitting) glances.
                    And he,
who has minded too much
and, overwhelmed—memories
at him troubling still—
stumbles into things,
simplicity a light upon
his face, breaks into smiles:
that bottom purity, blowing
ever more strongly, greets
the world from which it's come.

The Visit

Paris, Winter

To paint without a model,
shun all visits so that what one wants
to do cannot be interrupted or distracted,
as though the many strokes were someone
drawing near, the putting down of a landscape that cannot be till it composes
itself like a woman combing her hair,
touching up her face, arranging her shawl.

And then the lover, straining
at himself as at the distance that
intervenes, appears. The evening begins . . .

the evening began early, often shortly
after morning (which, plunged sputtering
down the well, bucketed back again
in a clatter of pots, the cries and smells
mixed in the courtyard, burst against
the walleyed window), in our scabby room
nearby the Luxembourg . . .
                              the rain
would soon be lowering its boulevards

and fountains, upstart there to launch toy
boats with furry boys and grandpapas
marauding golden coasts of smudgy Africa

till noon, bustling up beside the hedges,
in its shadows light upon the couples,
restive as a clutch of pigeons, flapping
out a crackly sky, full speech, around them . . .

you and I feel bare; our English dangling
like any bottomless pitcher over there
or what one might try to say to a world
absolutely deaf (and yet, we think,
if only we talk loud enough . . .), we huddle
in our room.
              Still this so-wintry page
looks English back at me as much as French.
And while you shiver in the crumpled bed,
I try by rubbing words to rummage out
a fire, at least one smoky morning ember,
a mumbling bird.
              I have, you know, learned
how to paint without a model, how to risk
no visits, many times O long ago.

II

                    Cambridge, Mass., Summer

To paint without a model,
shun all visits so that what one wants
to do cannot be interrupted or distracted,
as though the many strokes were someone
drawing near . . .
              and so the evening begins . . .

the evening began early, often shortly
after . . . no, I know that will not do

(what's Paris to the backwood likes of me
from tribes remembered best for kitchen-middens),
not that setting, not its tense, not all
the cries and smells.
                    Though they a moment
might have bellied out that someone's breath
as flotsam helps to ruffle up a flood,
they were, especially to French as skilled
as mine
            (and anyway perched now in Cambridge,
Mass., for all their clapped-together, clapboard
churches, as much my state as the Puritans':
the garbage, spewing out of cans, in steamy
stench an Indian prince, haloed by flies,
remarking it no more, no less, than if
in Paradise, droning their own mass),

too self-engrossed.
                    The someone drawing near,
under cover of this clatter, by the cast,
the grandpapas, the boated, puffy boys,
already in their play halfway to Africa

(somewhere, it is true, along that well,
in one room or another—shutters fastened,
still a deeply searching smell seeps out—
beside the bureau and a foundering bed,
the chairs, awry as with a gale, one guise
of him appears and, eyes glimmering
among the tears, blood spit, is happily,
absorbedly at work),
                        reflected in that
rain, each fountain spouting him, the maples
too, the shady glints the couples quarry
in the bushes,
                slipt away.

(Outside,
a hullabaloo: machinery, shouts. I listen,
drop my spluttering pen, dash out.

Before my door a main, clogged with debris
yesterday's hurricane swept in, has burst.
Watching the pleated water row the street,
as though at last the sea had found some
one small vent, I think of all the showers,
noon and evening thirsts, the flapping sail-
loud sheets and shirts on lines, washing
down the drain.
                        By now the giant crane—
a man with a white flower at one ear,
a skinny kid beside him, its quick brain—
has eaten out a crater in the street,
and four six-footers, heads around my knee,
with cries and thigh-high boots are sloshing
through the glossy mud.
                        A flurry of kids
like flotsam tossed up on the little flood
eddies shrilly at the curb.
                        One tries
his homemade boat along the gutter;
it throbs at once to water's impulse
and its own, then merrily bobs as though
days out on the high seas.)

                        Again that someone
slips away.
                        And I, like a cave dweller,
squatting in that old familiar smell,
mixed with the dump's fuming a sniff away,
his damp flint hunting fire, company
he loves so well
                        (the hulking, aerial
shapes he daubs on crooked stones, like him
who lay long months in clammy dark, heaven

flaking in his eyes),
                    behind façades
of odors, outcries, mad towns crashing by,
you fiddling in a corner, more and more
at home in Bach,
                    I huddle in our room,
waiting for the words, struck countless times,
to open, let the genie, burnt-match-black
and hot with incense, treasure, out: let me,
Eden-deep and sweeping-past-desire, in.

III

New York, Spring

To paint without a model,
shun all visits so that what one wants
to do cannot be interrupted or distracted,
as though the many strokes were someone
drawing near . . .
                    and so the evening begins.
Once more the stage is set, the properties
of night, so thick with wall in wall in wall
and bending to the page the stars are muffled
like the reassuring common faces
of the day.
                    Yet there to be completely
open, nothing on my hands, no help,
no pre-established passwords, nothing but
my innermost, most desperate need,
                              the some-
one drawing near, deftly as a woman
touching up her eyes with brush-strokes
that apprentice to their purpose light,
my look, the rain's legerdemain
                              (I feel,
I hear the flowers stirring, birds behind
already coming, combing out in flocks
fat, multifoliate summers),

open so
that in these lines what, taunting, passes
daily haunts and shapes, exultant
through the cast-off nimbus of a name,
nakedly appear.
                    "Terror is not French,"
Rimbaud said. Nor is it rustlings, siren,
savage, of the bush, a bug's argot,
the strange, lost mutterings of tribes
long dead.
                    Yet who shall say by way of beds,
the mirror with its making mouths (nacreous
cries submerged in it, the flesh still greedy
in the far-receding waves, moon giddy
as it dips in sherry, eyes), what does
get said.
                    Three apples, lustrous in this bowl,
plumped out as a speech: that cocky maple
at the window, blathering its head off,
full of country matters still: the rain,
running in and out its own Spenserian
exercises, blueprint of a wordy summer
crowding one small bush,
                          these, as I paint
without a model, risk no visits, express
themselves, and so consummately, so plainly
what they are, no record can be made,
nor need it be.
                    But what about the whispers
from next door, the voices burrowed in me
also, murmurings too close to hear?

        "A marching on the floor above,
        below, those in cellars, attics,
        boarded-over, mumble only
        hot, taut glances as they wait,
        the days one dark, for who knows
        whom, the sky lit up with friends

and kindred, echoing through sleep,
their hearts the thud of shovels,
earth, slapped into newdug holes."
                              Night,
once freshest air, heaven itself come, candid,
down to breathe with us, has turned into
a sealed-in cave, one wall in wall in wall,
a grave sodded with graves, till even sky
seems underground.
                    And sitting in this room,
one of many thousands like a Chinese box,
rather than these roses, apoplectic
as with your heart's blood, the walls' pale idiot
staring, havoc you desire, shearing
through the rooms.
                   Inside this city, gypsy
city going up, collapsing, like tents
pitched in a desert, how can these words,
burrowed into, save?
                     Do we not brush
the roaches basking there, the lordly rats,
the corpses heaped, their bloody whimperings,
as in these walls?
                   Listen. Familiar names,
the breathing hived, lost tribes, sound up again.
The ungainsayable honey-breath of spring,
your silvered glance, as cool and penetrating
as the rain, bursts through the dust and lights
on me, stirring birds and flowers, towing
multifoliate, fat summers.
                          Faces,
haloed in their touching innocence,
the reassuring common faces of the day,
whatever sweat and weariness, repeat
through crow's-feet indefatigable hope,
the child they keep, the child they keep on
being, shining more and more for every crease,
so bless this life, the thing I try to say.

I, for a time at least, by these as by
the hungry words invoking them past speech,
am spared that final visit, its one cap-
ping stroke.

IV

Annandale-on-Hudson, Autumn

(the voices burrowed in me . . .)

Anywhere they happen:
in this learned light now, ripening
through autumn, as though the mellowing
earth had finally imprinted itself,
a gloss, upon the quiet air,

as on the straw-in-amber-
bright pine-needles, matting the little
footbridge, anywhere they start up,
transported from a many-placed,
a many-timed remoteness,

breathing out a young
Egyptian morning, like the Nile brimmed
for its glittering rigs that seem
to bear it, there, surprising
as a passage in an old,

familiar book, frequently
reviewed, yet deeper now. Unfolding in my flesh, incognito, they travel,
waiting for me, feted in a look,
a phrase—this butterfly,

an eyelid long forgotten:
sunbeams, cleaving the dovetailed
trees, the laughter of my desert-wander-
ing friend and, far behind him,
in him, those who dared

the Red Sea and a desert
also for their dreaming of a land
sweet milk and honey—speeding, waiting,
to speed me farther on my course,
sufficiently looked after.

V

                                "But that's,"
she said, "more farfetched yet. There is,
it seems, no stopping you. The scene
you sketched, electric in its promises
and threats, you haven't used. Instead you
introduce another scene, another, still another,
topping that.
                 Whatever happened to the woman
shivering in bed? Was she the one who
worshipped at her mirror first? Or to that lover,
smart in terror and delight? The evening too
they might have reveled in?
                      Gone, all gone,
and scarcely touched upon. And you impressed
with palming off a lot of garbled copies,
each more preposterous than the last, copies
of a lost original; no doubt
a fake at that!"
                  Don't be so sure. That woman
may be you, you the more she changes, changing,
always more the same, much like the face
one finally comes to.
                Out of all that squalor
piled on squalor—no ancient cities built
on cities better—I would show that scene
and in its very shiftings,
                    show it fresh
as a new flower, proved, improved perhaps,
in each transplanting, unbetrayed by thought
or what it has been through, just like a mirror,

polished by the world of pictures flitting
in it, bountiful for its own sake alone.

The scene, well traveled, is unfolding, crisp
as ever, crystal parks and dapper, swift-
paced boulevards, the traffic civil, movements
of a woman, weaving through our steel
and glass, mirror-fluent, rain . . .

    and then the lover, straining
    at himself as at the distance that
    intervenes, appears . . .

The Last Day and the First

1968

The Last Day and the First

The stocky woman at the door,
with her young daughter "Linda" looking
down, as she pulls out several copies
of *The Watchtower* from her canvas bag,
in a heavy German accent asks me:
"Have you ever thought that these
may be the last days of the world?"

And to my nodding "Yes, I have,"
she and the delicate, blonde girl
without a further word, turning tail,
sheepishly walk away.
          And I feel
for them, as for us all, this world
in what may be its last days.
And yet this day itself is full
of unbelief, that or marvelously
convincing ignorance.
          Its young light
O so tentative, those first steps
as of a beginning dance (snowdrops
have already started up, and crocuses
we heard about last night the teller's
children quickly trampled in play)

make it hard not to believe that we are
teetering on creation's brink all over
again. And I almost thrill with fear
to think of what will soon be asked
of us, of you and me;
                      am I at least
not a little old now (like the world)
to be trembling on the edge
of nakedness, a love, as Stendhal
knew it, "as people love for the first
time at nineteen and in Italy"?

Ah well, until I have to crawl
on hands and knees and then can crawl
no more, so may it every Italian-
returning season be, ever the last
day of this world about to burst
and ever for blossoming the first.

Caliban Remembers

I

Might
have gone with them. Might. To be—
I heard their scheming—a strange fish,
stranded on land, lurching in shadows,
a monster they, tormenting, make.
No one for me. Not my master's kind
with perfumes stinking, auks at courting.
Nor to me true friends those two
I fell in with.
Oh fell in with,
a horse-pond for our pains, and over
ears, scum sticking to, thick scum.

"Putrid fish," all scoffed at me.
As if, from king on down, they did
not take their thrashed turn in the sea.
As in the way they reached this shore.

On such a day—moons marching by
my marking time—sat I out here,
sat, shading me, beneath this cliff.
The sea, one blinding wave, bulged round.
The sun had soaked deep into it,

into each bush, each tree. Had soaked
into these rocks until they shook
with light.
              There—I fished then too—
a great wind suddenly blowing up,
foam in its mouth, a bloody shriek,
that boat.
              Again and again surf broke
on it. Yet sparkling everywhere,
a blaze that, sizzling, blazed the more,
boat, gliding over this cove's jag rocks,
rode in. By then, for lightning's rifts,
one wave hot after me the sea,
I scuttled off, got me to
my sty's dark cleft and, glad at last
to have it, hid.
              My rod dangles,
once more sways the waters, swelling
from the line. New shadows come,
noises I hear past what such brooding
high-noon brings. Hummings out of the sea
and the air, out of the woods?
              Long tides
ago, I remember, hardly remember,
there were others. Low voices, rough,
could find me out, prod me, please.
No wasp's bite sharper, whirring through,
no grape-burst sweeter. Vague at best
now, like the name he'd knot to me.

Yet things I have belonged to them.
This gown, a giant ringdove's rainbow-
downy hood, I lounge in, tatters
and all, once my master while at magic
needs must wear, with that rod fishing
outlandish cries, their creatures in them,
from air and sea.

Lurked among books
he left. At times, efts in heaped leaves
as out of sleep, they pop. Yet as I
bend they fade, day after day
farther away.
                        But next to my hand
this pebble, blinked at me, a trinket
it might have been, dropped that time
I stumbled on her dreaming here,
dazzled by her still, as her glass,
cast off, raised to the face, a look
flashing, says she's, passing, teasing,
by behind me.
                        Chalk-faced, hair
sleeked down, no otter's better, stalked
behind her, basking in her light,
so darking me who saw her first,
that Ferdinand.
                        How push back
this crinkle badgers brow?
                                    Witch she,
not my poor mother, I tweaked as ever,
as a jay its secretest feather.
And most, blood at the heart hopping,
dare I speak out her name.
                                    Sometimes
taste still—remembering billows body
through, delight battering—gust
of that liquor. Cloud-casked surely,
music fermented. Those two bidding me
drink, one gulp, and no more goading
for me. God I, the sky my gliding,
earth, everything in it my subject,
far below.
                        Now, if ever they were,
gone. Even my sleep, only rarely
whispering in it, slips free of them.

From the thicket, peeping, watched
the long ship I helped stow fruit, fish,
water aboard sweep out and silently,
its sails confused with clouds, folding,
unfolding, melt as though the wind,
seeing them go, blew merrily.

At first I also, kicking up heels,
scattered round their garments, linens,
books. At first. But after—find
again that whole belonging mine
before they came?—and worst those days
when I, a smoke, fume through my hands,
loneliness whelms me.
                              Had I only
his book's good company, that company
it kept waiting, perfect, on him,
humble the world, I'd lord it truly.

My rod, sprouting though it did
from the staff he thought forever buried
and I plucked it, swish as it will
to rouse the breezes, rustle the sea,
fish shaken out, fat birds, their feathers
fluttered brightly as their cries,
fares forth no revelries like his,
nor no revelations neither.

Times I'd welcome the old, heavy
chores, his orders at roughest irk,
echoed in cramps, nips, pinches,
hedgehogs packed and inchmeal wedging
through me.
                    Times they rack me still,
those pokes, side-stitches (feared at first—
my shivers mounted—he'd returned;
aches he had, all kinds and fit
for each part of the body, aches

he must have stuffed in hollow branches
sealed with pitch and as the music
from his pipe, as smoke behuffed
into the breath, at will puffed out);
and shapes they do in the dark, giddily
torching me that I slubber in bogs,
on mad bushes burr me, furzes clawing.
But now with no sense of meaning, no ape-
mouthing sprites behind them to mock,
not anger, only themselves.
                              Themselves
those plumes awag at the water's edge,
draggled through mire, flood, yet dry,
a play straight out of the spume?
                              Not those
from the ship again, untouched, a miracle,
unless the shine they sport be sea's
(my master bragged he kept them so),
nor straggle-heeled in memory,
but a dirt-glittering file, great bugs.

Well, what comes, more or less, I accept,
my state on the isle. Its flocks and herds,
its slyest creatures, these, as I pluck
for hides, food, feathers, tribute
also in their squawky cowering,
at least acknowledge me King. Tame too
as they never were for those. Long days
I loll, ruler and subjects the same.

Things I learned, it is true, some,
nag at me still, names that, shimmering,
as I would clamp jaws to, dissolve.
And the faces glimmered out at me
from bush and sky, tide-riding shapes.

Came on her in this very cove,
swimming still on her, whiter, rounder

than a wave dashed on the shore,
drops drying like pearls, open to the sun.
Then I understood his daily command:
"Stand upright, stand!" Upright I was,
knew at last what he meant by "Be
a man." Saw she was gone there, torn
out by the roots. Wish in sudden,
flushed kindness, pity, give her mine,
all.
    But tiptoed, manhood in hand,
to surprise her, completed while she slept,
as by magic—was it our fires,
crossing, drew him?—scepter quivering,
upright, he appears. Eyes blazed
on me, cares, it seems, nothing
I have learned my lesson, prompt
to obey.
        Fear he had I'd fish
his pond? Oh no, not fish it, stock it!
Who else was there to do her turn,
so save the day for man on the island?
Not all his magic, age, can angle
new foundlings, me more, out of air.
Mere thinking it wrings.
            Still his words,
crackling, strike me everywhere stony
if feelingful. One frown farther
I had been done.

II

        But hear that hiss.
Its skin atwitch, the sea would speak?
A rumbling scrabbles.
           And the rod
grows taut, throbs, humming, in my hands.
Some odd, mad fish I've caught? Haul
it up.

There, soaked, dripping,
thick sighs spluttered from it, bobs
a swollen, slippery thing.
                              Clutch it.
A book. That book? My master's prize,
the one he wished drowned!
                              Alive again;
inside its blotched pages, sea sick,
for all the sights, outlandish worlds,
it's gulped, the words, through fingers slither-
ing minnows, hop. Mixed in its spells now,
nymphs he cropped, nymphs and urchins,
romping, couple, splotched with purple
swirling.
              Clouds he called this world,
clouds and dreams (a sorcerer then,
a stronger, over him, mouthing things,
wording us, puffed thus into being,
browsing on our aches and rages?).
Such waking cloud this book's become.
Reading—fidgety gnat-words, flicking
eye—not hard enough!
                              Yet some,
their tails, flouncing, all I catch
as if plunged, the rest of them,
twinkling, into the sea or swamped
by smudgy ink, I nearly recognize.

Put ear to page, hear something, grumbling
steady, a power, far off, collecting.
His voice, is it, penned in the words?

This the book, the very one
he used, depended on most, most
to abuse me.
                  Master he may have been,
yet could do nothing without me. Not,
unless I, fetching sticks, patched fire,

rouse his magic, its highflown tricks.
Whatever his flights, had to return
to this island, his cell, me.
Never could, whatever his flights,
go back to his country till they came
with that ship. I only propped him, kept
as earth does sky, else dropped in the sea.

Why then should I not use it also?
Shake me out music, that brave host,
showering praises, presents isle-heaped:
luscious fruits flung from the trees;
liquors clouds, cask-big, split,
pour down, thirsty for my tongue;
fish pied flying in out of waves
as the sea itself, glistening, bows,
then at my feet stows dutiful ships,
with treasure crammed as giant hives,
their honeycombs oozing.
                    Maybe can,
why not, raise one fair as she,
a dozen, sea-blooms, wreathing her,
bent on one thing only, hooked,
dolphin-sleek, dished in the sun,
one thing: pleasing me.
                    Cloudy as sky,
bow-taut, is growing, better hurry.
Drape the robes about me, so.
Wagging the staff, take that half-
crouched, half-stiff stance, nose aloft
as though snuffling powerful scents,
the music working under things.

Now find the place in the book.
                    Here,
the lines most faded. Head nodding
right, then left, both eyes rolling,
yet lordly, words begin to twist.

And body caught in the sway, they sound
something like this.
                    (Never knew,
clever as he believed he was,
often through a chink I spied
on him mumbo-jumboing to air,
then jutting ear as if he thought
to hear answer. And was there something,
mutters, say the air's bright crest,
aflutter, speaking, speaking I
now seem to be hearing out of these
drowsy trees?)
                    Oh, could he see
me now, his lessons like his scepter
clutched, the earth, the sea, the cloud-
packed sky about to wake, how pleased
he'd have to be.
                    I can, mouth gulped,
almost repeat that rounded phrase
finished off in a hiss.
                    Lo, now, lo!
Even as I say it, darkness hedges,
crowding out of the sea.
                    Beware!
A lightning crashes, fire's scribble
scratchy down sky; and that oak, sky-tall,
falls at my feet.
                    Homage truly.
One twig closer and I had been ever
more crowned!
                    Wake that squall again?
Watching him manage it, hearing
out of it bellows, no beasts madder,
demons not (suppose more loosed
than he could handle?), shuddered me
through.
                    There, high on its ruff, the osprey

its spray, the cormorant beaking it,
muscular mist, and riding, gay
as a porpoise, a gull, in the distance
the ship bobbing that took them off!

Desire that: my master back,
she, the others, logs, fast rooted
where I dumped them, ache in my bones,
the play, I ever cast for monster,
slave, to be played over and over?

Oh no. Now this able book's mine,
my lackeys they.
                    Ah the sweet tasks
I'd conjure up for them as—standing,
upright, rigid, by, they glare
their envy's deadly looks—I lie
in my flower-soft bed, she, flower
among flowers, by me, mistress
to my least worded, far-fetched whim,
breath mixed with, winging, lilac, thyme.

And him I bid bring turtle eggs,
struggle through fanged briers for berries,
prickles too of bees he must snatch
choicest honeysacks from.
                              The others,
husked of rapiers, ruffs, fine airs,
down on all fours, the beasts they are,
cuff them, kick. Out of their yelping,
as master's pipe could ply a storm,
pluck music.
                    One bears me a bowl
brims rose-water, petals swimming;
and dabbling hands, on another I wipe.
Then order these pour ripest wine
down throat. Or "Scratch the regal back
with porcupine." Set on the palace

his book shows, "Scoop out that fen.
Put rocks over there. There. And there."
And, put, not liking it, "Put back
again."
        But as they, drooping, sigh,
their struts and frets, wildfire plots,
gone out, would I not let them be,
him most, most haggard for these labors
far beyond his years, and he, first
landing on this shore, enjoying
for a time what he found here, most kind?
As I enjoyed, a time, the silks,
the warmth and airs he (she more) soothed
against me.
        Best in the twilit cool,
as now, puffed from the earth and sea,
the shadows out of the deepening wood.
Then, he piping, I sprawled by,
the notes bubbling, dewy moonlight
vibrant on them, as in her eyes
glittering secrets of caves sea-kept,
she sang. And winds and waves, chins set
in their hands, the stars, leant down, peering
ever harder as darkness ripened,
also sang. One radiant sound,
the earth and sky involved in it,
soaked into me, I shook with light.

So he, sitting over me—great patience
he had, as I at my fishing—listened.
Points at things, making fish mouths,
stranger noises. And a mote
baiting my eye, a may-fly twirling,
whole day, if tiny, on midnoon,
prods with "Mind, mind!" till at last,
no salmon swifter thrashing waters,
flipped above the spray, the word,
in me erupting, pops from my lips.

Joy in him then, love like my own.
Eager to show me this thing, that,
bold for the blessing of a name.
Tales he unfolds with airs in them
from castles as from clouds that dances
gleam like waterfalls, beteeming
stately woods, by birds set off.
His books spread out before me, shared,
I learn to pin their swart bugs down.

A book, it seems, for everything,
for things that cannot be and never
could. Had one even showing me
and called, so it said, "Caliban"
because I fed, not less gladly
than on ants, on men. How could I,
no man being here? And think
of eating those, washed up, rotten,
worse than flotsam, on this shore!
To them alone such name belongs
who would, not cold, not hungry, kill.
(The name I had I never told,
with mother buried who gave it me.)

But best of all that warbling book,
written as on a cloud, about clouds,
the world so graved, growing, changing,
one thing into another, like a cloud,
its women turning, as the pages
do, into a tree, a brook,
a song. Who would have thought, with nothing
left of them, their silvery looks,
their voices, but the sighing of a leaf,
a rivulet, the hearer's tears
jet forth, the world seen newly
in their light.
                    But am not I,
not merely stone, such changeling too?

So she, in one day sped from childhood
stalk-thin, awkward, into woman.
What I became she could not see
but only heard, as I would sigh,
the same old shaggy husk of me,
as that god, changed, so the book said,
into a bull for love, must bellow.

Books browsed on as my own. All,
that is, but one and that craved most.
No matter how I strained, heaven
it loomed, mocking, over my head.
And that the book I saw him lost
in, sitting by the fire, listening
to its gossip, mixed with the jiggly
words, his stare outgleaming embers.
That tongue, so good at wagging, flogging,
little about him then but as it
jogs off on its own. And the eye
that easily caught me out, no eye
for me, a thing that never was.

Mornings too, quick to me earth,
the berries restless in their plot,
the sky as well, I know it time
to tend the day. And he shut away
as though, beyond those pages marked,
no light, no joy, can bloom.
                              Damned be
such book when world in lark enough,
in filbert and in plum, cries out
that I became a winged hearing,
lapping tongue, and those the ground-
work eyes and hands abound them in,
my feelings, ripened as they ripe.

Let him be buried in his glimmering
dark while I sprawl in the sun,

in busy, slow pleasure running hot
fingers over me. Or, plunging,
lounge inside the thicket, tickled
by the shade, webs buzzing, leaf-mold
rotting on mold, a wood-bug sometimes
gulped with a berry.
                  Long hours on
and into the night within my fingers,
under my lids, the daylight tingles,
tingle too along my dreams
those sizzling smells, the fruits as when
I munched on them. And he, after,
the fire gone out? Gray, ash-gray.

Yet that one book—now I have it!—
is it better than the world, telling
where winds are woven, snows, sundowns,
showing them being made, and played
out as its owner bids?
                Some god
must have bestowed it on my master,
else dropped it—as later he did—
lying open, wind-leafed, wind-sighing,
like this earth, and my master found it.

Time and place forgot, he wandered
in it, blissfully lost, the world
assorted, cherries, rainbows, beetles
boxed. So on this island all
the seasons at once or, as he wished,
seasons of most outlandish countries,
mountains in his cell and light
as clouds, tall mountains flaming round
the embers, goddesses too and sprites—
the show of them.
             But then he saw—
perhaps the days between the spells,
their willingness to work, grew longer,

harder, or he woke, ash-gray—
what empty dream he'd snared him in,
learned the lesson I had always known:
with that book to give himself, to dive
into the thrilling waters, chilled
at times, hard buffeting, this world,
this life is?

   Maybe, come back, stroking
and teaching again, his words mine,
I finding some he did not know
like new nests, crag-set, I could show
him, eggs speckled with writing brighter
than his book's, sly birds, the topmost
sky still breathing from their wings,
in their songs still, he'd once more trust,
entrust the isle, his rule, as mate
his daughter.

   May that ribboned thing,
filched my place with the logs, her fancy
also, drown, this time for good,
a delicate food lining fish bellies,
sweet between my royal teeth.
Then, who knows, she might, seeing
him at last so much in me,
like me the more.

   Or, better, let him,
soaked enough, grown scaly through
and through, yanked out, Caliban me.
If he, pale sprout, could supplant me,
why I not him? Three times as much
as his dragged, staggering poor armful,
he a king's son, I can haul.

Our names with their three syllables,
two mountains humping a crouched "i"—
Cal-i-ban and Ferd-i-nand,
Ferdinand and Caliban—
are surely like enough so that

the mouth which shaped out his with loving
breath, trill birds would stop to hear,
to mine could be as kissing-kind?
Ah, well, would she ever have—
how could she—loved a thing like me?

Why, instead of all that work,
those lessons, slow, dull, scratchy,
did my master, worlds at hand,
not turn me presto into prince?
Sea, fire, sky he managed
featly; but I too much for him,
earth magic alone could never change?

Never, as he sought to stuff me
with his learning, asked he me
my thought, my feeling. All I was
was wrong, to change. All he wished
was aping, my face wrought to look,
a mirror, more and more like his.

III

The book in hand, past teaching now.
Let's see, squatting under this rock,
what rubbing these, the last two words,
together does.
            That grating stink,
dredged up from grotto bottoms, bogs,
sunk under the sea.
              And swelling out,
choking the air, one racketing cry.

He's back, overseeing me, making me
do what I do. Or Setebos
with his accursed crew, sneaked in
at last and most to devil me—

who else is left to feed their hate?—
for being driven off.
                    A crack
as though the earth is splitting!
                              Out there,
lit, the ocean spouts. One monstrous
fish?
        No, upright, like a mighty
man in flashing robes and roars—
if only he came back how gladly
I would give this book, myself,
and all the isle to him once more—
I see it, see his city, so he
called it, climbing the skies, its spires,
cloud-piled, the gardens sauntering
with gilded fountains, songs torch-lit,
while far below dark fires rage,
the swamp on which such city's built.

Like torrents crashing over a crag
it burrows every secret store
of me, one shattered ear.
                    Now crumbles,
tumbling drags the outermost rim
of the isle with it!
                    My doing? Not done
a lone thing yet brings me one crumb
of joy; no music—only this howling,
sky clipt open, trolls my name.

What if, the salt marsh flushed and pounced
on me, I move the moon, the sea
rushed over the isle, I among mollusks
down there, for sharks a crunchy music?

Ass enough that time I dreamed
I could, with those two clumsy sots,
set me free, get rule. Master

I called one, god, licking his foot,
and he, for all the sack in him,
not mire good enough to cake
my master's boot. And I believed
he'd bottled moonshine, music, himself,
the moon's own man, dropped with them!

Oh lessoned I am. Off with the gown
and break the wand. Before this book,
more than ever my master did,
reigns over me, ruins entirely,
drown it again. Never wanted it
in the first place.
                              So let it sink.
Dissolved into the restlessly paging
(seems to be reading it), gurgling sea,
the nymphs and dolphins schooled by it,
it may, sea-changed, sigh out its message.
As now.
                Whatever his tempest brought
about, this one washes me clean
of them, blundering on their tottery
two feet (upright they pride themselves
on being!), in broad daylight bethicketed,
wilder than night. And all the time
planning havoc.
                        Why so foolish
as to toss his power away and, naked,
return to a world bustling with men,
his brother, my silly crew, repeated
a thousand, thousand times over? Expose,
as well as himself, his dear daughter
to infections, plagues, far past the wiles
of scummy ponds!
                            Devils they said
haunting this island. No least devil
till they arrived. Not all the toads
and frogs this island spawns could quell

the viper in them. Devils he sailed
away with, devils, waiting, hordes,
to dog him all his life's last days.
Think of a world, an island like this,
swarmed with them, their schemings, brawls!

Winds blow over me, the crooning
night air, free now, full of nothing
but its own breath, serenades
the locusts chirr, scents of the sea
and this my island, twining with
what stars are pouring.
     Yet, not burrs
snarled tighter in the hair, they cling,
that manyed voice, as in a sea-
shell, ebbing, wailing, far inside
into my ear.
    Fingers remember
the bowl they brought, his hand on it,
hers, the water gushed forth, sparkling,
laughter, words. I polishing,
how it gleamed in pleasure, overwrought with my face.
     Its carvings music
swelling to the eye, the finger,
from the pipe the piper on it
raises who is blowing out
the rounded, cloud-big, smoky sky,
I enter it, the little landscape
centered in thick trees a wind
in fragrant waves is wreathing, wreathing
me, shapes watching.
    Him I see,
see her approaching. Eyes smart,
fingers tingle, taught sly snaggings
of silk, as eyes are caught by her
skirt rustling, the drop of her lids
a deafening tide in the blood till I,

battered as by that liquor's gust,
for the flooding over me drown.

Oh no, not that again, not me
gone in the dark of too much light.
Not bowls, nor touching words, to push
me out of me.
                    There, smash it
to the earth, the dust it after all
is. And through its shattered pieces,
him and her, those others scattered,
I tramp free, free as the air.

But free of what? Not lost, all ebbed
away, as water from the bowl,
for that they would have taught?
                              Too high
he rose, high-handed reached past earth
into the clouds he sacked, while I
slumped, an earth, below.
                         At last
he changed his mind, chose man, the life
that all men lead, a magic, dream
more than enough?
                  Preferred the bowl
no less at breaking, robes faded
and faces, dyings, their plots too,
their hates.
             But most that momentary,
everlasting human touch—to touch
Miranda's hand again! A queen now,
joy of children throning her
as they, shrill, ruckle round her knees?
And he, does he live still, sometimes,
head shaking, bent in some forgotten
corner over an old book,
muttering maybe "Caliban"?—
the fearful, wide-open risk of it,

feeling, as men feel, as men call it
real.
      Preferred. As I finally learned,
little though he knew it, learned
to love him, going. And do.
               No matter
how I burrow in shadows on shadows,
leaves thick and dark mixing, dark
from inside owl wings, bat's screechy
darting, my cave sealed off, I stick out,
prickly, listening.
          How I long
to hear once more those me-completing
voices. Come back, would cast me
at their feet. And yet . . . alone, alone
as he must be, loathing, pitying, loving.

The Eighth Day

Twilight lidding the fifth day,
did He steep His hands in them, self-
reaping riches newly won, His powers
proud to see themselves adorned
by what they did —
                              the horned, lowing
as they moved, a forest headlong,
into balmy slumber like His stabling
hands: the serpents, no more twisted
than their manes: the condors,
                              bedded
in their puffed-up feathers, curling
by the lambs, with vines festooning,
consummating dark: winds also, water,
nodding to their hum?
                              And still
the coursing in His fingers of that
thoroughfare, the lovely and com-
mingled traffic burst from Him, stars
too dazzled
                  in that all-talking air.
Having made so much, each a witness
to His growing mastery, sufficient
to itself if not to Him, He must
pass on,

          press through these others
to the last, the one in whom the rest
would congregate, who, gisted of them,
would at once be able to salute
the thoroughfare
                    with names that,
murmuring, afford them room to mine
and bruit their teeming, secret wealth.
Accordingly, this sixth day, upright,
strove to be,
                    the manly day that,
harking back through bird and snake,
tree, water, star and wind, would feel
these words, those hands, so resonant
within he must break free.

A Letter from the Pygmies

Dear Whoever-You-Are-That-You-Are,

Whatever chance this has of reaching You,
I write to bring You up to date.

I cannot, little as I join them
in their skills at hunting,
undertake Your tigers. Rarely
do Your lofty auks invite me
to the confabs of their aeries.
Pastimes Leviathan delights in
never has he offered to share
with me; never has he proffered
island back or cove-snug belly.

Still there is the cat Hoppy
who, whatever our blandishments,
as he cannot drop his creaturehood,
claws flying in his pleasure, takes me
some good distance into Your creation;
dew starlit on his fur, the fields
wherein Your wonders grow he smells of.
And when, unblinkingly, he fixes me
as though he were upon the scent

of rabbit, mouse, or other friend,
I know the instantaneous delight
of terror. So elation finds me
in the chickadee that bobs
upon our thrashing window-bush,
skullcap awry like any plucky Jew's,
a Job in synagogue of ashes, cries;
as Hoppy bats the pane, it never
budges from our fat-packed rind.

In short, though there's a scheme
afoot to blow Your ark and all in it
to smithereens, to pitch a cloudy,
climbing tower will convert the earth
into one tomb, I know by feelings
craning, preening deep inside
the ark's still riding, riding high.

So from time to time, what time remains,
I'll do my best to keep in touch with You.

Faithfully Yours,
Theodore

The Ultimate Antientropy*

"Unity is plural and at minimum two."
R. BUCKMINSTER FULLER

Whether one paints five Helens
after some much experienced woman
or develops one, his beau ideal,
from the five, most lovely, untouched
virgins of Crotona (such Cicero's
account of Zeuxis' purist practice)
or laboriously patches her together
cheek by jowl out of all the women
he has shuffled through, is not
their end the same?
                              So even he
who will not let the name of Helen,
or woman for that matter, be attached
to what he splotches on the canvas,
refusing to be tamed by recognition—
for he claims he paints a painting,
not a landscape, apples, females—
deems he's plucked from out his head-

* According to Norbert Wiener and R.
Buckminster Fuller, "Man is the ultimate
antientropy."

long brain and brush a universal
as it is a most unique,
                              concrete
past any momentary model. And though
we may wish to celebrate the fleeting
or applaud the theory as it lords it
over its bleak and boring product,
Zeus, we recall, laid all (this every
time) his eggs in one small basket;
the consequence, in the most famous
case, was a Helen who inherited
her papa's quality
                              most jovial:
being so promiscuous, so radiantly loose, that we have hardly seen
the last of her. The sparks her eyes
shot forth are seeds that will not die.
Men far flung still warm their hands,
their hearts, and more at the thought
of her as at the Troy the flint
of flesh against the tinder of a god
produced.
                    Helen, it seems, is more
herself the more she's reproduced.

The Life of . . .

for Bill and Dorothy

I

"So there we were stuck
in Alassio all that rotten winter
in a rented house, no one around
but puffed-up Germans, and nothing
to read beyond a pair I can't abide,
Boswell and Johnson, the latter worse
than his crony.
                                And nothing to do
but struggle on through that wretched
Life of . . . . How I loathed it!"

II

"Ah, my friend," I say, "that's what,
more or less, it always comes to,
one book to a customer.

Storms clattering through their lines,
some, if they've the time for it,
wonder how they'll ever learn to follow,
let alone unravel, their chaotic plot.

Others, it's true, are luckier:
richer text, with pictures, colored,
every second page and gilt-edged, bound
in buckram that's the latest rage.

But each of us, like it or not,
is stuck in his own Alassio, waiting
there, flopped open."

III

                              "Actually,"
my friend's wife now breaks in, "after
the first two summer months, after
the Germans left, the gaudy decorations
nailed up on the shops for them
pulled down,
                    and the Italians
gradually appearing, rotten winter
and all, we grew to love the town,
admit it.
              Why, whatever the weather's
ludicrous fits, just our garden alone,
with its crazy, tangled, nonstop blooming—
      roses, geraniums, and the rest—
through shattered bottles, cans, and every
kind of litter.
                Or those narrow, dark,
malarial streets at the end of which,
on our long walks, the sea glittered
like a blaze burst through a tunnel.

And that's not all. Have you forgotten
the forlorn little fishing-fleet going out
each night as we went to bed and, at dawn,
returning as we woke,
                            threw open
the shutters, and watched behind it

a red heaped up on the creamy water,
the sun rising, as though, towed
in, part of the catch?
                    And a bit later
too, once we learned our way around,
the mountain that we loved to climb,
looming over the town and high enough
with its paths twisting to the top
so that one seemed to see—
                              a new day
previewed there, just as it was forging
forth—eye to eye with the moon."

The Life of . . . (Cont.)

for Irma

the poem is speaking

"Since, after one quick look,
another friend of yours dared say,
'This poem seems to need some resolution,'
I, a kind of Party of the Fourth Part,
stand up to insist
                the poem is
satisfactory. Some lines—the eyewash
about a new day, etc.—are a little hard
to swallow. But at least you resisted
gab of chariots,
                Apollo and his
nags chafing at the bit and all that.
Even if you couldn't, as ever, withstand
your blather about books. What's more,
one whiff of Germans
                and off
you go like an old horse to a blaze.
OK, don't blow up. I know you deserve
some praise (living through so much
revision, I had almost forgot)

for blotting verses in Part II
after 'each . . . flopped open.' Lines
about people like books, suddenly hurled
across the room, 'with dozens pulped
or fed into a roaring fire
                            that . . .
at last the words all crackle.' Sure
the title fits, just right with its dots,
neat X's marking the uncertain spot,
for those millions
                            razed in smoke.
In any case, I am here to offer exegesis:
like the trio in the poem depending on
one another as their talk composes
it or, ever stuck
                            in their high-
wire act and in the hazy air of new-
comers to the show, the pair your friend
abhors, you stand on them (so you
and your woman spin
                            through space
with no rope, no net, and least of all
trapeze beyond each other). As I now do,
the latest overlooker, telling you
how much you supervise
                            the rest.
And it continues, like the shuffling
pages of the sea that in different light
(and by the lights of him who looks)
look differently."

Far Out, Far In

I

What we go out for
we often do not know,
though some are lucky
thinking that they do,

like those priests
in their white cassocks
diving into the canals
of Venice after the cross,

or those explorers
plunged, perverse enough,
through swamps and jungles,
most at home when lost,

and those luckiest
of all perhaps, gone out
simply for the pleasure—
limbs set, mind—of going,

as from this beach
a stand of grown pines
closes in, protected past
that by a mountain range.

II

On stilt-like poles
nets, dangling, shimmer
in the wind coral-crimson,
minnow-golden, seaweed-

green—in the fish
one wishes to lure one
must anticipate varieties
of taste; nearby glass

knobs for floaters
that craze the sunlight;
also mats adazzle with
fish laid out to dry;

and boats in whose
high-pooped shade men,
women and children sort
the day's many-sided catch.

III

But now, newspapers
spread out on the ground,
rainbow awnings strung
up from the trees,

the picnic, a festival
of swimming, begins;
food taken, some half
awash in the frothy surf,

a few, up to their chins,
go through the motions
of swimming, their arms
a lazy mimic of the waves.

IV

But there, far out,
near the bigger, seagoing
fishing-boats at anchor,
one ambitious swimmer

shows off her skill.
Hair flashing as the sun
catches, already low,
on arms as on the water,

fish dart to her
and as if excited by her
presence, her performance—
no less than their habit

at this hour—frolic,
in pairs, sometimes
in schools that seem one
rainbowed curve, leap high

V

into the air. Then
even as the day goes
down, sinking somewhere,
a glittering treasure,

at the bottom
of the sea, the swimmer,
done with swimming,
by some artful strokes,

sure of herself
as of her course, returns
to shore. Whatever she
was after, as she stands,

dripping yet serene,
a last reflection, on
the sand, she has, for
a time at least, found it.

VI

So, night glinting
round in mottled waves,
two, swum far out, far in,
through one another's arms,

desire briefly routed,
drift upon the moon-
lit current before sleep.
And as the mind goes out,

exploring memories,
sensations like deposits
in the veins, the far-
out, lively places where

the body's lain, elations
gather, sun and wind
and water freshened, able
so, intrepid, to remain.

Lines for an Ending

for Joseph Frank

Now this letter is on its own,
catching at me at unexpected times
like a kite high in the sky, torn
loose from its tether (or is it
a wing blading the sun?), like
a single patch of snow in a bush
that seems at last to be struggling
free of a long, involved affair
with winter.
        Once a flock of soft-
fleeced yearlings paused to pasture
in its lines. And for a sudden wind
as of danger, the acrid smell perhaps
of gathering fire, panic took
them. Or at times an intense calm
would settle on them, and as though
to a shepherd's pipe they would troop
in a docile order
            to lap at
a lucid pool in the letter's center
or cluster round an altar for one
of the seasons' rites, winter to be
sacrificed to and fed. One by one

no doubt and then in numbers,
pounced on by a passing, ravenous
wolf or harried by neglect, the flock
diminished.
               Now this letter lies,
a ghost, in my hand. I open its dry,
rasping pages like faded, sighing
leaves, and a wistfulness stirs
as in a temple whose sanctuary
is long deserted, whose spaces echo
with lean, empty winds. What troubles
most is forgetting, the poignancy
of passions once everlasting.

A Midsummer Nightmare

It is the waking . . .

Maybe now it's come to this,
a tale patched out of countless tales
some idiot is blabbering, remote
as it can be from its original.

Bessie, loose at every seam, flaps by,
backed by glossy deer, their glazed
looks fixed into the woods or on those
plastered others, idolized creatures,
in her more or less real frontyard.

We might as well admit that we
at last have come to this—the core
of high-toned stories, of curvetting
lords and ladies, sleek and furred
and fit as cats
              ("cats nothing, rather
flittery tilts of gnats and midges,
courting sun")—
                the stink, the boredom,
nameless under the moment's gilt,
their Maytime-buzzing fame.

                                   Are we
not proud to think ourselves the first
to see hell's plenty in a furnished room,
in Helen's charms the fly-blown brow
of Egypt, germs at seethe beteeming her blood's Nile?
                    ("We sound, in me
no less than thee, the very base-
string of humility.")
                              Yet still
the race by its ground sense commands
respect enough to make me say—

and if already mutants, they will find
their necessary lingo, fables, place:
no less impressive than the virgin
and the unicorn disporting,
Bessie queens it through her animals—

whatever setting and green, ragged cast
the roles must put up with, the play
goes on.
                Inside the obscene clatter
local voices, silences
colloquial, like little lolling
waves in wallowing storms, hold forth
as ever: cricket, river, mountain-
lofty trees.
                ("You think there is
no havoc here, no looking after
rights, good cheer, of catastrophe?
This giant tribe that troops, so grave,
soft-footed ants like shapes embossed
on urns, with their heroic dead
are laden down.")
                        Perhaps the time's
come round once more for trotting out
that graybeard of a musical,

"The Battle with the Centaurs," sung
by an Athenian eunuch to the harp.

Old horseplay never long suppressed—
Cretan, Trojan, or the downy god
flopped, rutting, into slubbered duck—
those shaggy beats, black leather
jacketeers, half man, half roaring
motor, now break up the wedding,
the barely held decorum.
                              We'll none
of that? No lout, a hempen, playing Prince, and no falsetto fumbl-
ing at the strings?
                        O let the muses,
thrice three muses, appropriately
mumbling in a row, dumbfounded,
mow at the birth of poesy
in those unlabored in the brain.

Brief though their toil, their fame,
may be, some ten words, ten days, long,
in all the work not one word apt,
the roles forgot before the play begins,
and still I have respect enough.

The will—whether the Will of Avon
or the Passaic's goose—is here:
muddy the mouth, an ass's frowsy head,
a centaur's cleft and clumsy hoof,
the yearning that is love still blunders
into loveliness.

Mount Washington

> At Mount Washington, in Tuckerman's Ravine,
> Thoreau had a bad fall. . . . As he was . . .
> getting up . . . he saw for the first time . . .
> the Arnica mollis.
>
> EMERSON'S "THOREAU"

Insert 942 of the poet who views
and reviews his work from summer's *aperçu*.
The day had been a day, a genius,
to study out in intimate detail
the earth's sweet, diverse plenitude of June,
itself exactly mirrored in that multiple
response.
       And now, night-lidded, day's so many
ages amaze themselves among their dreams
as dateless snows are adding lofty stories
to Mount Washington,
                the one—"highest
in the NE United States, real quality
for skiing"—friends are urging him, afraid
of heights, to climb.
              Had he not crept on hands
and knees—from childhood up: the thorny bluffs
his gang explored—along La Scala's gallery
while Godunov, mid-career, appointed

like the candelabra, lit in its own pride,
giddied him the more.
                              Afraid and, as
a guidebook later told him, rightly so:
"The first effect of standing on the summit
of Mt. Washington is a bewildering
of the senses at the extent and lawlessness
of the spectacle. It is as though we were
looking upon a chaos. The land is tossed
into a tempest."
                              Inching through the Alps
    by train, he felt them, churning, scramble him,
    this in their greatest wildness with a logic
    of their own, serene for very fervency.

But he has now lived long enough to know
he need not awe himself with icy heights.
Wherever he may be, a full-fledged storm
spreading anonymity, and he is lost.
Or sometimes caught flatfooted on most daily-
seeming ground, the stars at midnight striding
that low street, and there abruptly stirs
a vertigo good as the proudest peak's.

    A flower, basking in itself as in sunlight,
    let its perch be pinnacle or ditch,
    plucked, can instantly unlock the pit,
    sprung up, impassioned, slavering, of Dis,
    sky plummeting as by that tiny ledge
    the body is.
                              And so, his pages crawling
with revisions, queries to himself,
and with his doodles, intricate waystations,
he tries to find a certainty inside
against such dreadful falls.
                              Nor, as he views
his work, is he averse to plying tales
of other travelers who climbed this way.

Kindred especially as they had spent
their lives striving to map part of the course,
map often nothing more than accurate
report of perils, loss, and being lost,
scale map in color of catastrophe,
and yet because they had been here a light,
provisions cached in sudden crevices
along the slope.

INSERT 942

        In New Hampshire, crisp
despite mosquito-fretting notions of July,
a full moon close as any fellow New Englander,
the crickets choral in their book of airs
as though a grassy hymnal hummed itself,
the poet thumbs *Ein Bildungsbuch für Kinder*
that his host had brought from Hitler Germany.
The first of its kind, put out in 1796
by a friend of Goethe. A most serious magazine
with tidy drawings of the matter-of-fact
wonders of the world
                        (the sometime text below
now in bookish German and French, now also
in an English never heard on Anglo-
Saxon land or sea).
                Fish ripple through
his fingers, swum in their own radiance
as in the foamy shoals flipped pages make,
names flickering,
        "mackerel, pickerel, perch."

The poet, squinting, cocks his ear. Might he
not overhear, among the moonlit murmurings
his window frames—the lake, moon-piled, impatient
mica mountain, brimmed into the mirror
by his side—these piebald things?
                        And so

he is amazed as flowers seem to leaf
and, sniffing, laugh through him:
                                        nonchalance
    in roses, frizzled manes. But others ruffled
    as—not to be told from—crinolines.
    One roisterous, all ruddy nose, for drinking
    its own wine.
                            Narcissi, self-absorbed.
    And then a twinkling edelweiss atop
    its precipice, as though these pages heaped
    them up to mount it that it supervise.

    Much like that bird of paradise that preens
    as it goes teetering through painted eyes,
    a fan coquetting.
                            With great moths set off
    like sunsets, mazy dreams, a map each one
    of the Babylon informing summer
                                        moonlight
    of this night, a someone blinded as he
    looks, gets mixed up in.
                            And choice volcanoes
    about to wake, bouquets most artfully
    arranged.
                    There, bigger, huffier than the rest,
    "Vesuvius," with people by, watching
    from low balconies.
                            Several bending,
        robes a burnt sienna,
                                    especially
    now they blend with the poet's studious shadow
        (few pleasures like the looking down on mountains
    happily in hand.
                            So only as mists,
        roomy as clouds, had cribbed him had he dared
    to scale storm-battered Snowdon.
                                        With the ease
    of dreams the mists like curtains parting, scapes

dissolving into scapes, some cows float by,
sudden pastel vistas, autumn clearings,
prim as album scenes, the leaves compiling
light upon each other:
                              see that intrepid
mountaineer, S.T.C., but on the top of Skiddaw,
in the vales of Quantock, best in one of many
paper-drifted, frost-at-midnight rooms,
hot on the tracks of Hegel, Schlegel, Schelling,
Fichte, all in turn after the edelweiss, and not in a cloud-cuckoo-talking,
smoke-baroque salon),
                              New Hampshire and
the poet intent on this High German view
(perhaps the eyes look up that once set here,
the scenes, asleep as at the mirror's bottom)
of a medieval dusk,
                              toward others, backed
by hairpin arches, churches fly-eyed, blinking
on devotions, assignations, plots too sly
for any prying,
                              strollers in the wool
of ripened peach and pollen, volubly browsing
in a homespun moonlight, someone strumming
a pandora,
                              as Vesuvius, twitching
in its slumbers, sputtering, snores along.

Meantime, roused in a lower corner—
                                        the poet
thinks he sees their busy, black-cowled buzzing,
this highlighted by the gnat that perches
next to them, a more than life-sized, glittering
angel, stunned by what they're at—
                              flushed
on them the luscious vines they, tending,
            trample,
            and their sheep, well-fleeced, two monks exhort

a woman, sketchily got up, a touch
too rosy if offhand.
                And cheek by jowl
the mightily scowling "Giant of Ecuador,"
decked out as noble savages should be.
Swashbuckled, ruffed,
              the spitting image he
of George—so wigged and snuffed as—Washington
crossing a replica (the artist's version,
adapted when he scooped it from the Neckar)
of the Delaware.
         Foot on the prow
as though, for all the cakes and floes beside him
like a glacier's brow, his hand is eloquent-
ly drawn to plant the Stars and Stripes Forever
on Mt. Washington.
          There, hard on the General's
          heels,
those fabulous louts, half Indian, half cow-
boy, trooping in.
         And blurring with the poplars
(the paper, peering through, as though it were
brown twilight's air and of a forest too,
confused with whatever woods were meant;
nor can this moment's moon make clear how many
voices since, how many tramping feet,
have sounded through.
         The poet thinks he senses
their retreating and can draw them back
as he divines the future already marching)
as they did for Burgoyne and his Hessians
until they fall on them, lined up, a whooping,
bloody fall, the red coats redder, glinting
in the sun as in the flash of guns
and powder-horns.
         Across the page more apes:
the four above seem reasonably real;
the fifth, however—

            some inbetween, a sport,
        flaunting its cocksure tail much like a fur-
        below and drooping, gold-red locks that look
        a German spoof at newest *haute couture*
        (did not Marquis de Lafayette inject
        a Gallic note into the coonskin war?)—
    "shows itself plainly through the long, thin
    & almost horn-shap'd nose from other apes."

The poet knows attention must be paid
even to the unlikely likes of such
as to that daedal kin as well—their amours,
Weltschmerz, rituals, cuisine—that can
not be unless aired in our words:
                                call them
atoms, gnomes, or what you will, the Great
Migration teeming through our dreams, the thicker
they swarm the more invisible they grow,
much like snowflakes confounded in one snow.

So, in reverse, that starry race, the farther
off they are, sped to us from a world—
a book?—that's gone, the homelier they glow.

        Like these "colibri" or hummingbirds whose hover
        held, the wink of snows, dusk wading trees,
        circumfoliates plumage.
                        Particularly one,
            "the Tree-creeper, ivygreen, with a falcat'd,
            trifurcat'd bill."
                        In its quiver moonlight
    is shaking loose (only a leaf or two
    between such slippery seasons)
                        the Russian Winter
        of 1776 or thereabouts that flocks
        like flakes from pages otherwise brown:
        sports "of the most belov'd divertisements"
        of the Slavic people, viz.:

"Fig. I,
The Mountain of Ice,
wooden scaffolds, about 18 yards high,
one side a wooden slopeness, cover'd
with pieces of ice, & sprinkl'd with water,
on which the lovers, being always numerous,
or seat'd on little sledges, or standing
on skates, with such violence slide down
that they continue gliding, & for many
miles,"
   far as the poet's fancy, savoring
this ice, no sherbet sweeter topping autumn
fruits—
  he too, despite his hating heights,
has clambered hand in hand with a companion
up a glassy mountainside, blood tingling,
eyes bedazzled with a noble white
  (who knows whose gazing lightens over them,
  its breath ignited, buoyant, in their breath,
  that crags once more become hot gamboling,
  so paced by them, the Jungfrau passionate),
and then, sledge or skates or no, swooped down—
darts out
   "on the snowy way prepar'd below.

  Such artificial icy mountains are
every year in the carnival's week with loving
care constructed at St. Petersbourg
[in Peter the Great's wintry Sommergarten
Mars & Venus long ago deferr'd
to the Cossack snowpair, sparkling as long days
& nights they twirl out capers]
      on or near
the Newa."
   Now the poet, certain he
can hear the grapplings, happy first as games,
children tumbling round and round in drifts,
sees lovers' volleys, mixed wih others, graved

along the groaning ice of lakes, the years
enrolled in riots, massacres.
                      And still,
like all the stars in revolution gleaming,
fires rollicksome puffed cheek to cheek,
flakes, confetti whirling, dress most savage
winds in furs, the rivers, famines, prinked
out so, stark degradations.
                         There, just below
the Mountain of Ice, snow huffing like a
      samovar,
are swaddled folk, selling refreshments,
"a mead of sugar & pepper, to be drunk
with or without milk, & Russian gingerbread."

Is this the spot, the poet wonders, pondering his page, this point, its dotted line,
to plunk the snow, lugged from childhood up,
that makes the world a mountain-top, a lunar
sight, immutable?
                As then, no less,
when through him, like a native shivering
in his tent, a fever roamed that little room,
its wall-flowers, wild through the glaze, maze
quite practical for its hallucinations,
good enough to grace the proudest crag.

This the spot to press the child's first flakes,
memories embalmed in them, the rose
of Chartres not more crystal-clear, or what
a tapestry sought to capture in its spinning:

faces spinning, kindergarten faces,
pouring out to storm him in the playground,
chalky teachers packed within a word,
loves opening like furtive, scribbled notes,
one face among the rest a flowering
that time can only intensify—

the dead,
his mother, harried spirit, freed at last
into the winds; his father, bolted past
the failures of the flesh in one swift hurtling
by horse; and his dear friend, a poet, veteran
mountaineer at least ten years ahead
it made good sense to follow.
                    (Had the heights
    not sprung up, loving and at once available,
    inside his gaze, blue lookings from the snow,
    the piercing sky, as mountains blaze, dawn
            molten
    down the sides, that time their lives, their vague
    if urgent, lovely fates, loomed over them,
    awaiting their triumphal climb?
                    So they,
    breathing in their hopes, airs of the much
    loved great, longed for their earthly paradise
    on a forked peak, floating with the stars.

    Yet paradise was almost theirs in knowing
    those, compact of wing and song, also
    depend on them, the moment's topmost mount,
    for being as for exaltation.
                    This
    in the city man has built and restlessly
    rebuilds, adding lofty stories to,
    nomad as the most desperate heart could wish,
    a wind-swept Alp tossed on itself they
            wandered
    day and night, admiring its spired
    citadels, its frosty lights,
                    the range
    spread out far below that he must shoulder
    even as it, dizzying, props him.)
And follow though his friend, having danced
out on a precipice much like a sparkling
rapier's edge, plunged into an avalanche

and now, two decades dead, grows light—
between the pages of this basic book
no one will open, ever find, past mining
itself in some all-giving flower:
                              voices
ice has locked, climbed out, climb over it
in crocus, lilac, columbine, and clear
the cry the hyacinth remarks.
                              In front,
          as the plate has it, by a line of stands,
          a fur-hatted, fat, mustachioed vendor,
          having already tasted of his wares,
          wildly, a nine-day-wonder astride the world,
          gesticulates.
                              One cocky edelweiss,
          these snows its fathomings—
                              like an Alpine climber
perching on a stock, the poet stalking
via pen onto the slippery hillock
of his creased and tracked-up manuscript,
then out into the air where eagles loiter,
stars in undress, much at home—
                              looks down,
          a summer's *aperçu*.
                              And so the poet
sees that we, whatever crag or ditch
we stand upon, by might of gaiety,
by feeling's cubits, top earth with itself,
its latest blossoming.
                              "Through this," cries edel-
          weiss, the daylight haloed round it, stars
          nearby, "the nights yearslong, the storms and wars
          the world at winter hardly seems sufficient
          for, my unique taste has brewed, brewed me
          my single honey-home!"

A Russian Lesson

to Boris Pasternak

I

Hunched over your pages,
I tighten my eyes as though
I might, through the pitchblack
of this language I don't know,
via the tracks

          you've left
in it, benighted as I am,
by concentration penetrate
the swirling sheets on sheets;
such struggling

          seems just
right, the very core of poetry-
making and something you, sitting
deep inside your Russian
winter, must have understood.

Others, hearing, would scoff,
as your time in its frenzy
hounded you: a grown man, playing
with words no one can understand
while the world is burning!

Oh it was terribly hard on you,
hard as on our Hawthorne say,
hiding away in his mother's house,
scorn noisy in his mind, haunted
by the living
                as by the dead,
the piratical and the proud,
so unbowed by the ruthless fates
they seemed to push them past
themselves
                as into his thoughts
till he was scarcely sure
he had not, like the creatures
he had long pursued, turned
into a ghost and disappeared.

                II

But I have you to keep me
company; even in my feeling
lost inside this rigid winter's
black-and-white, as through
the reaches
                of time and death
you've gone into, I count
on you. With your old peasant
women, workers, students, country-
men you've come to stay.

The light you shed like a lamp
in a distant room, shadowing
long, frozen lanes, and the light
things cast out of themselves,
glowing in your words,
                            flow
over me. That light reflects
something, a bounty, of forest-

deep firs, lining your house,
snows too,
        falling through them
as through bottomless space,
and in the field across the road
the little cemetery, snug
in blue-bright wooden fences

with zigzag crosses, planted
in the snow, and rose-petaled
paperflowers, children flashing
beyond it as they swish by
on a pond.
        I count on such gifts,
your great anguish and your loving-
kindness, reaching out, to see
me through, to help me find
you.

III

    And this that follows,
a wreath composed of leaves
gathered from your rare garden,
trimmed as I transplant them,
is where we most meet.
        For
having seen what those who hated
and feared, as well as those
who thought they admired, did
to you,
        catching glimpses of
your sad face through the barbed
wire of translations, I know
that till I try, by giving
whatever love and skill
        I have,

to let you be in your own poems,
but as they come alive in me
and claim as they release this
larger life,
    you cannot be—
nor I with you—triumphant, free.

This Gray Age

(after Pasternak)

Had I known it then, really known,
before I began this wretched scribbling
(my dear friend, older in the business,
even as he was about to leave the stage
forever, did his best to warn me;
but how, caught up in that dream, fame
and its glamor, could I understand him),
known how deadly the lines of passion,
clutching at the throat, would be,

I would most certainly have scorned
all this desperate fiddle, this dressing
up my feelings, I all absorbed, in high-
falutin craft. One fumbles away at first,
hardly aware of the price he has,
in effort as in fevered pain, to pay.

But now the act is done. Instead
of gags and jugglery, glib cleverness
that hogs the stage a moment, this gray
age like Rome, bored with mere sideshows,
wooden daggers, bags of spouting
pig-blood, cries out for the real thing—
that the actor, falling in earnest, die.

When passion is the play, play,
alas, is over, and the one who long
had sought the spotlight, in it at last,
finds to his astonishment that he's
not mouthing art, the phrases he's put
through their measured paces a thousand,
thousand times, but the fatal, final lines
of earth itself, life, destiny unbudgeable.

Wunsch-zettel

Oh, no, it is not hard to be alone
the whole year through. Though I at times almost
forget the sound of voices, laughter, alone,
in any true sense, I am not.
                         The seasons
visit; memories. If well attended to,
new crops they bear, surprises like a shoot
that, overnight left out in dew, bursts forth.
Solitudes ripen, silence, from these mighty
days over my woods and waters browsing.

There, you see, behind the house, my mountains
watching, sensitive to every whim
of light; on the other side, the mountain quick-
ening my lake; and, far beyond, the Alps.
To share their presence you think one needs to be
with them?
              I have the good, long winters here
when snows, big at this window, fill, as though—
just like our skiing days—high over my head
they loom, the Jungfrau's summit reached. Great
     climbers
too we were, my husband a champion,
you know. Then down, earth rushing to embrace,
the body air that through me morning flies.

And made of eyes, peering into this room,
the woods look round, as through my working hours
stride little life and large. They know no fear,
the birds and squirrels, the rabbits and the moles.
One noon, horns sparkling in that sparkling day,
four deer. Bowered among the parent antlers,
the young frisked so the lawn and this bay window,
like a sunbeam flashing, seemed to leap.

But come, let us go upstairs; for there
the study is, an even better view.
My staircase knight a little frightens you?
A creaky ancestor who guards me from night's
mares. Oh I would welcome a sprightly ghost,
but ghosts at best, alas, homebodies are,
by waves unsettled.
                  The carpet came with me.
In its deep quiet one walks as in a park,
and straight into the past unrolling, ever
by me those I love.
                  This is my room.
Hushed, no? A den with moss and rushes lined.
So you see, sitting here, free as I am
to my work and to myself, maybe I—
your visit's kindness I do appreciate—
can make you understand not I from everyone am lost.
                  That top shelf bulging with books?
The garden books I've turned my time into,
best telling how, how long, I've striven for this:
a garden to be implanted in each mind,
with fruits for others, blessed community.

This edelweiss pressed—between the brown leaves
of childhood's *Wilhelm Tell* I keep it—smell
it please.
                You catch the windy mountain fragrance
clinging to it still? My leaving this house

it recalls for me—in fifteen years the first—
to visit Europe again.
                         To Switzerland
I went, some six weeks of a tiny village:
the world's lost young, war's handiwork, transplanted
as in one proving-bed. Yes, others there were,
children villages American money
began. Quite so. Pestalozzi named,
after the great teacher.
                         Why did I go?
Because of all my work they called on me,
as you do now, to teach them gardening.
Children, think of it, Polish, Russian, Greek,
poured in from everywhere. Looking up to me,
their hunger made them one.
                         No, no lectures.
For so mixed a group, the other teachers
as well, of every land and adult age,
what could one prepare?
                         So then I used
the moment, out of both sleeves magic, and hoped
for the best. Nature, I told them, can be
trusted. Though how they, plucked from the wreck
of Europe, could trust to trust me I do not know.

Starved looks, the Greek children most, fixed on me,
I did what I could. Expression, you know, one tells
by eyes, the upper part of the lid. But those
had saucer eyes, at least as round below,
in each disaster heaped, huge emptiness.
And then on next year's wheat to bid them live!

There in Switzerland those wintry weeks,
high in an attic, peaked its roof among peaks,
cold, alone, a cot, a chest hand-carved,
one candle weaving.
                         By candle I love to work.

To sit near it, before you the night, the whole
great night at once around you, faces leaning,
flowers, to the light. Then all we are,
the selves of dream and wake, together flare.

By candle—in Germany for darkness all we
dared—I wrote my third book. A night unbroken
composing it. In itself gay, though for it
waking hours and my daughters suffered.
Books and buds so pressed their only out-
of-doors while I tried, in vain, to dam
the growing terror. In vain.
                                        Midnight knew
no stop. That May the first a fever-glisten,
droves of relatives and friends—my grandmother's "Forget!"—boxed away in vans.

True, time has passed, much time like heavy earth
turned up and piled upon that time. So then,
and in that children's village, living so,
round us nothing but their needs and the good-
natured elements, soon signs of change
like crocus tips in frozen clods peeped through.

Here, let me show you that time's first harvest.
As European young ones used to, for me
they drew a Wunsch-zettel, a Christmas wishing-
list. And think of it, not one of them
had ever seen a garden. Drawings these
of dream desires, flowers they would plant.
All this and this just one week's industry.
These French drawings, such bushy frolic greens,
such candy reds, are best, yes?
                                        Already
I had reached them? Havoc still flickering
in their eyes, in their hands earth began
again.
              To see them watching their hands, skills,

hard won, surprised in colors and shapes surprised,
like petals spread to cup the sun molds them.

These—a little cramped and pedantic, no?—
the British children, with no sense of gardens.
Gardens you thought deep-rooted in the English?
Not in these, mostly raised in London,
cockney, the underground their home.
                                        Proclaimed
themselves better than the rest, far better
than the Polish, for they had a place
to go back to.
                    At the Christmas party we made
with hymns and games, the Britishers, as though
by signal, their caps sideways, rushing in,
started to push the Polish from the room:
"No place you have, none here!"
                                        What did I do?
I was not slow to disgrace their fists with shakings.
Then futile I thought. Beside such as my own,
the shame and wretchedness we grown-ups relish,
how could they feel shame?
                                Still the faith
my father, no step from the creatures, had
and took as air for granted stayed with me.

Till three I said no single word. My mother
worried, but the tinkling goat-bell father
tied to me soon reassured.
                                "That child,"
he smiled, "only when she can put her words
in perfect sentences will speak."
                                        What other
namings needed I? Clear voices they were,
the animals, wings, petalings, voices
like the sun in heather loud. Each day
I took him to our flower-beds to show
each fragrant task the seedlings were performing.

Then, dew still wet, fists clenched as though inside
a seed I bore the world, I came to him
and, opening, to show the sod I clutched:
"An affection for our fertile earth, dear father,
I have always cherished and will." Amazed
he was, as much as you, and pleased. Later
he learned my sentence had been read to me.
Still that I chose to memorize, no other.

For words, as they first blossomed in our breath
from picture-books, soon wound into my life.
Already cuttings I tried to keep in beds
of pages to look at when the winter came,
though, turning to, I found that while I slept,
wind calling, kindred, they had slipped away.

Stories too, striding through our endless days,
echoed round the garden that the birds
over their chirpings seemed to nod. For her words—
our aunt, loved before the rest—bent over
us, turned all into a fable, the daily
far and lofty, the lofty near, like stately
gowns by ploughs and geese and hayricks twirling.

Even now, as I glance at my curving
path, out of some grand tale jogging here
it seems, with sweeping chestnut plumes like knights
and ladies cantering.
                              A dream it is,
mere revery. For little here can imitate
our first house.
                              Oh, yes, this one is fine enough.
The past I've done my best to reproduce.
But how compare it with that other's court,
dense orderly rows of chestnut, or the pool
carved curly dolphin flanked?
                                            Then I was twelve.
The garden rang with boys, with games and stilts.

At dinner we hung hawthorn wreaths on a poplar,
shaggy colts to wait for us.
                              To wait!
Like all laughter all galloped away. In the dark I woke,
many trembling nights, as though the dark had sickened.
Not all my tears could warm or comfort it,
not though those tears, like bread crumbs waking
in the moonlight, sought to take me back.

Still even now my aunt, and near the fire-
place, in the standing mirror that I keep
by me, appears: the first terrible time
a grown-up cried.
                    Her visits had been jaunts,
her wildfire haunting me. Always she came
with flowers that her face, whenever thought of,
loomed a flower among flowers.
                                But see, she stands—
far in winter it is—with her back to the fire,
hands thrust away as though she hates their touch,
this body that betrayed her into joy, pride
struggling, my mother turned to console her.
And down her velvet cheeks the tears, spiky
with the fire, glitter.
                        "I cry," she cries—
the gates in my first garden clanging shut—
"because crying, as women ever have,
is all I can, as though the ones I cry
from those long gone were little different.
Oh not to Him I cry but that the world
can do without them as though they'd never been."

Reasons enough: her son drowned on an outing,
and just some months before her husband found,
slumped by his manuscript, his hand fixed round
its "finis."
            I could only blame those two
for carelessness to wish those tears on her.

The heartless ways of boys! Men too I saw.
The new wound started up the old, her son
not even killed, as schoolfriends soon would be,
in numbers, we then thought, past tears' accounting.

Nor those more easily wiped out, as we
one summer day might douse a hornet's nest
and listen to the crackling. Our friends,
whole streets and neighborhoods, all rumbled off,
in smoke a moment tracing the wind's design.

And though her husband's dying and her son's
were terrible, I could not know, no more
than she, how comforting they would become.
For theirs not deaths to tear apart the house,
the garden, and the world.
       Still vastly opening,
deepening, the flowers stood. I sought them
as if the days, the years, in them might ripen.
At sixteen to those much older I taught a garden
class. People shook their heads: "Of such
a noble line and happiest when grubbing
in dirt!" And looked at me as though they thought
out of my fingertips the weeds must sprout.
At eighteen I wrote my first garden book.
Five now, five paper greeneries, behind me.

And they go on. The games still race in them;
like giraffes the stilts lean over ivied walls.

How carefree once we were, free with brook
and sky and bird, the covered bridge, with boys
and girls, joy led, about to skip across
into the meadow where the loaded wagons
creak with summer.
       Bit by bit the windows
shut. After such as these, my grandmother,
my father, and my aunt, by the very gaiety

they taught overpowering in the pity
they implore, who could reach out for more?

You are right. The dearest faces stay:
the little ones, themselves like candles lit,
the air around me wafting their warm breath.

Surprising then that I worked with those children?
But one must take care how he touches them
lest like powdery flower, butterfly,
the cool blue flame, the fragile breath, be smudged.

Though many scoff, I know what community
beyond mere place and time such efforts mean.
Community: Comenius first and then
a host untold, monks in their monasteries,
Rousseau, and even Goethe, toiled by me,
the rain and sun so bending, no less busy
with me frog and bug.
                              Note that brown drawing
over my desk. Dated 1840 it is.
Precious itself, far more for what it shows:
Friedrich Froebel's venturous first gardens,
in the village of Blankenburg in Thuringia,
with little children playing, tending the beds.
And in the background can you glimpse the steeple
and the housetops overseeing them?
At once Herr Froebel would implant in them
the sense of being a part of the community.

His lovely word, *Kindergarten*, shines.
But his hopes for it, his work? The rose's breath
often in my beds divined his love.
Him and the others, my gardening's choice wreath,
my father at last, my husband, by my side.

My husband, eyes fixed on some far distance—
glinting in them the loftiest, fresh snows—

my hyacinths shaken by his swift passing,
strides toward the mountains.
                              Always he
must go beyond the last peak others dared.
Oh I can understand the need, to plant
a flag, my flowers, and to stand in a place
where no one else has stood, as I my feelings
first, then in a spot least promising,
those children say.
                         How well I can remember
earliest winter dawns, the first wind, sprung
as from my sleep, a mist on it, the pond's
calm breath; and there in its pane, sheet-thin,
as with night's starry back besilvered, first
I was to see myself, the only one,
even as the sun sucked up that pane,
my look, my breath into the air. Oh well
I understand.
                    After that day I never
skied again. That day as ever I heated
water in a pot over a bramble
fire. Returning, pride flushed on him still,
his dip among far crevasses ice-cold,
into my hot, voice ringing out, he'd plunge
to enjoy the burn.
                         The water cools, then turns
to ice. In it no face but frozen crags—
my tears, wherever I looked.
                                        Moments that mountain
thawed. Through its briny flood a prow
would jut, grating on new shores.
                                             New shores
that wait upon the olive branch restored.
Wherever dark earth is in time I know
flowering can be. In those small villages
again already Froebel was, you might
say, flowering. In no easy way be sure.
Yet overnight pinched faces seemed to lift.

Yes, quickly in the village such circulating
with the fragrant things taught everyone
good cheer. Strength also, what hands can breed.
A humbleness before the mysteries,
nature at its workings past our reach.
And not alone great lightnings, flooded storms.
The smallest, wood-deep bud, only by shades
and butterflies attended, the light hidden
in it already dreaming, loveliness-
to-be, from blossoming is not held back.

And patience as to know not every weed,
some keeping for the flowers water, to be
plucked. Faith too, as after furious hail,
nature calming, a bed can be scooped up,
replanted, healed.
                    One night the Polish beds,
and more completely than a storm could do it,
were destroyed. Complain or cry they did not;
only their faces, of a calm inconsolable,
turned from me. Again I tried; it worked.

At night, after we saw how over us stars
prevail, in darkness best, stories I told them
of famous men, their trials and mighty triumphs
through such trials, read to them from books
savory as the worlds they, born of, bore,
more piercing not the taste of the sassafras-root.

From that it was an easy step to move
to gardening in other countries, ranging
from the Zuider Zee, Salt River Valley,
far back as the Hanging Gardens of Babylon,
the Pharaohs and before. At last to Eden,
the Great Grandsire, nodding through the rest.

So human beings in their aspirations
sweetly stay alive. Not only in the stars

do men engrave their names, but artfully
in earth's perennial habits.
                           Think of having
flowering in your garden—as those children
did—at home, indifferent to time,
the proud Narcissi: Horace, John Evelyn,
Sir Watkins' Crew, Franciska Drake, Lord Wellington,
and all the other gallants, ladies, full-
blown in a single bed, broadcasting subtle
messages, their scents, to one another
on each passing breeze.
                           More definite
than we, these flourishers, enrobed in better
than belief. Attended to, new crops
they bear, surprises that, just overnight
left out in dew, burst forth.
                           But should we nod,
weeds overwhelm, the lusts, the greeds, man falls
a quick prey to, through all the growing rampant.

In the middle of the night Germany so,
a world around us crackling. And we fled,
seeking a brandnew garden for my children.

Out of harm I saved this, their first piano,
their earliest lessons, father's music-stand,
those mollusks, gleaming on the table, bent
to their own songs, stronger than iron cities.
But, like sea-rocks imperturbable,
their siren voices always sounding stranger.
Not long my children valued them, the lessons,
the piano, as though, one with the mollusks,
muttering still that lost intolerable world.

And so it goes. My youngest writes to me
in German; though a young lady now, her German
grows, grows daily, worse. Amusing the errors

creeping in from English. This to explain
the few letters she sends.
                                   No, I do not mind.
It keeps the little girl she was alive
with me, as in this glass I spy her still.
And spy her more as more and more my girls
depart, as though their growing, women now,
were growing away from me.
                                   It may be so;
our first flight may have set the pattern.
One with that early world they seem to be,
a world like ripped-up paper dropped behind,
like bread crumbs scattered many a bird had gobbled
long before my girls could grow enough—
have memories, and in one spot, would house
their senses lighting and their first delights—
to be, whatever the land, secure within
themselves.
                   Well, maybe later they will find
some reassurance—quite so, like those children
in the village—landmarks, in my books,
a home.
                   Meantime? I wait, welcoming them
whenever they'd return. Meantime, I gaze
into the glass.
                   No, not my crystal ball.
But sudden surfacings in it; and sometimes
too, when I look out this window, I am
amazed, as though a stained figure had leaped
into a painting, strange and yet belonging,
the way one shade can rearrange a scene.
Or on the brightest page a shadow strays.

Ah well, the summers thrive, days honeycombs
enhiving all, on woods and waters browsing.

Then, when the world seems a triumphant blaze,
the fanfare of some lavish conqueror,

a loosening sets in, a letting go.
Each day a leaf strews at the tree's foot
till leaves in sighing companies speck sky.

And soon, the winds a blinded swirling like one
lost, the snows months-long as though a wilderness to cross.
                    And yet each flake a footprint—
his who sought to climb to the end of snows?
So lost, their end he may have shared, to melt
into the skies.
                    The summers through him—
the gaze of—rise once more, a hyacinth,
as this one on my desk, with his last cry,
ensnared, contracted in a crooked streak.

But how can I release, as out of books
this sprig of edelweiss, the loved ones spelled
in leaf and reed and flower? Say how much
can one preserve or smuggle through in leaves,
stamped with all one's love and grief, cuttings
kept against the cold?
                    Never to come
again, not though I plant and nurse ten thousand,
thousand hyacinths, spill all my care
upon small growing things.
                    Why one could slash
through all of them and still not reach the dear ones
they are living on.
                    You may be right.
By being themselves and nothing but themselves,
to our outlandish deeds impervious,
things make, and cleanly, our lives possible.

Five years ago I visited in Germany once more,
an old school friend most ill. The hospital,
a huge new metal block, stood in rubble.

At her window I saw, and all alone,
a tree. And instantly by the bole's slant
as by the twist of the branches spilling shadows
over the wall, I knew: the slender poplar
of the limb on which we used to hang our wreaths.

After fifty years all that remains
of my first garden. The fine, spacious court
now one bristle of geometric lines,
like those black ledgers father used to keep,
figures—gardens too, he, smiling, said—
I could not follow.
                   No, I'll not go back,
not though you ask me to carry on my work.
Froebel would understand, and Goethe more,
seeing what they had striven for so lost,
Germany, the whole of Europe, changed.
Of refugees, uprooted ones, alas,
there is no end. Nor place to hide the grief.
The birds' sweet cries ensnarled with other cries,
that soil for countless churnings, burials
on burials, too spent to bear new crops.

Here? Nothing so close, so tangled with
beginnings, nor so glutted yet with ends.

New gardens? During the war far as my lake
I plotted land. But the war itself engrossed me.
And after I gave over, let nature take
its own set course. Plants only in the house.
As much as I can tend.
               But now, the sun
descending, we are come to my favorite part
of the day. Above the lake twilight, gathering,
brims, the mountains as at birth.
                  How good
of you to say from out the children's drawings
the colors seem to flow.

Over the mountains
the woods have crept, and like the dusk they sweep
to cover scars. And let them sweep. No, no,
I'll not go back lest scars, discovering
new strength, like hungry mouths ask more of me
than I can bear.
One never knows, I know,
from what surprising source, this hyacinth say,
deep cradled in its petals, sorrow springs,
wayward as our joys.
One night—if night
it could be called, for the late summer sun
had been so strong it had beglimmered thickest
shades and brought in after-dark a rush
of voices, wings, loud wagglings round a candle—
at my door a sudden clattering.
There,
as out of earth, ice-bolted earth, pawed free,
forelegs uprearing, mouth enfrothed, a horse.

Maned with midday blossoms, is it winter,
dark, denied and roused from its stiff bed
of snows on snows, my childhood mount, chafing
on this moment's peak at being lost,
yet come for me at flood?

The World Before Us

1970

The Witness

Something must be left
like music broken
off in a flute's throat . . .

they showed me, my friends,
the little green figure
they, camouflaging each other,
had dug up out there
before the famous shrine.

It caught her eye first
that her eye became
a drop, a gem, the latest
thing wrought by that long-
gone maker and his bit
of metal.
            Showing it,
the scene rose up again
on the tide of their breath.

I, listening, was suddenly
out there through many
a distant, ancient vista
I once had trodden

under in the new dust
of my past,

out in a headlong dance, hand
in hand with someone
panting at my side,
the great ear
pointed to my ground,

engrossed in this,
the latest passage, most
outlandish, of its music.

The Heir Apparent

My father's ripped pants,
my grandfather's bulging shoes.
Get used to the patch that covers
the seat of one, his knees
stuffed out with prayers and a kind
of crawling, tight, tight, on a proud man.

And bundle the toes
for those miles of walking
factory floors that turn the world
into one tiny spot with girls
at machines like machines until
his satchels, bursting, spouted laughter,

delights to prank
a country fair. And hair
spun out of the web of my mother,
hair like a nest hatching eggs
of her anger lighting on each thing,
a desert ensuring the eggs' eggs' future.

And plying them all,
bright threads on a loom,
playing them out, then pulling
them taut and, having bitten

off frayed ends, knotting them in,
my grandmother who never admitted America;

she lived in it
as she had lived at home
and traveled over the dizzy sea:
a few familiar rooms, loud
with people needing care, needing
her, oil spread upon the troubled waters.

And I composed of these
and the many nameless, my walk
a bit cramped for the bunioned shoes,
the baggy knees, the hair full of snarls,
but my grandmother tidying up, serving
hot cups of tea. With lemon.

Sealed In

You, as if to say,
"I can't take it any more,"
turned your life over to us:
"See what you can make of it."

And like the crabbed note
you sent, written late
in your life by madness
ascendant,
       a cry I hid
beneath a clutter of papers
jamming my desk, we tried
to bury you.
       Now lost
though it may be, I feel it
like a bit of radium, what
I used to fear as a child,

something so powerful,
so alive, it must eat
through all the substance
of the world.
       Plucked
out of becoming and kept

at best, so we assumed,
in the amber flicker-

ing of memory, you were,
we reassured ourselves,
a kind of perfection now,
like some dead language.

We could not see how much
this Sanskrit, say, lay
at the roots of all our talk.
You who should be
                    gone,
from hard and glassy, shell-
like, scarab wing-cases down
to dust,
            instead fly faster,
whirring, in the taut sky
of our breath. Neglect
cultivating you,
                you grow,
wild harvest, to surprise us
in the latest turn we take
as though you were,
                    not only
waiting at its end, but
the force that makes that
turning possible.

Black-and-White

for Nadine Gordimer

Father's Hungary? Mother's Philadelphia?
Poland of her parents? Reading where I
was born? Behind them all Jerusalem?

Eden's had to come a long way, the dusts
of myriad lands mixed with its dust
in its trudging.
              And I, a momentary
paste compounded of this sifted ground,
groping for the Adam all but muddy
in me?
          I will not undertake
some dream, not be even in revery
as the Africans call one who has gone
to the white land and returned
a "been-to."
             No, I will lean
heavily on this ground under my foot
that is my ground, know the taste
of ur-man in this local mouth,
food seasoned with his spit,
                    words
also, splitting open, cooling waters

or the spices of them, long sealed in,
at once transported as my tongue
can savor and my bowels respond.

Responding too, a wave that woman
by her skills of look and touch,
her body close, is loosing in my loins,
I anointed, king, in my own oils.

And in the sweat upon my brow
those living, salty words are written,
sunlight flashing on them like that
interdicting sword.
                          I am a man
as red earth, black, composes, am,
once blank, a page ghost for its sights,
the black now scribbled ever heavier,
blotches more and more the text.

Am I a black man with a white skin
time shows the thinness of, a white man
hiding red-black blood below?
                          Those first
fountains, waters sparkling with those
first lips, surge in me through wind
and blinding snow.

And Still Another Troy

for Harold Donohue

To open oneself
and to open though the smoke and rot
keeps choking in . . .
                              there you are,
a city inspector trudging on
your downtown rounds, and a Greek luncheonette
owner spots *The Odyssey* in your bag,
of which you wrote: "I'm finally making it."

And, puzzled, he stares a full minute
at the first page. Then abruptly
his high school Homeric Greek,
"the minimum for what is considered
an educated man," begins to work

as he lights on "Aithiopes"
and in pride and delight points it out
to his Negro partner: "the word for Negro."
There you are,
                              as you put it,
in this your poor beleagured city, making
one of those occasional contacts
between your worlds.

And I wonder
at the Homeric phrases lighting up, the few
that now at last, in your words, reach
out and touch you,
                    open so that maybe
some night in crumpled, whispering sleep,
the young hoods in you helping, shopkeepers,
whores, those words, a troop of them, leap
out of you and at you;
                         instantly
in your dream, yet more than dream,
your world flares everywhere
as though a goddess
                     were striding
through it. And the understanding then,
"that true Athenian" you call it, at last
remembered fully and fluently, how
will you bear it?
                   And but yesterday I said
to someone, "New York's a Troy burning."

"Yes, But . . . "

for WCW again

There he was—having spent
the night with us, the first
time away from home alone,
terribly frail for another stroke,
his dreams still shaking him—
his fame steadily leaping ahead,

and he complaining to me,
struggling just to be somebody,
expecting me to comfort him!

Manfully, if with a bitter sense
of injustice, I did my best:
"Why, Bill, you've left a good
green swath of writing behind you."

And he, in a low voice,
most mournfully, "Yes, but
is it poetry?"
                    That years ago.
Only now I begin to understand
the doubts necessary to one
always open, always desperate

(his work's honesty, spontaneity—
work nothing, life—depended
on it),
        one too so given
over to the moment, so lover-
faithfully serving it,
he could remember or believe
in little else.
           (Some months
later Frost would visit,
older, sturdy as an ancient oak,
unlike Williams, who could not read
to the end of a verse,
                intoning
his poems well over an hour
with tremendous relish, then
standing on his solid stumps
another hour batting it out
with students,
           no doubts shaking
him and few new leaves breaking
out of him.)
          And only now,
the years, the doubts accumulating,
can I be grateful to Bill
for his uncertainty,
           can I lean
on it, lean more than on all
his accomplishments, those greeny
asphodel triumphs.

The Ruins

At first these works may have been
painfully poor, slapped down as they
were by someone who had never seen
a painting before or who took out
his hatred, strong to madness,
on these daubs.

          Then there's
the possibility that somewhere
near the middle their artist tired,
thought of another livelier project,
or out of sudden panic, pain,
fled the spot.

          On the other hand,
they might have covered over
masterly works, the way a child
or a wild young man must scribble
his signature, a bushy blind mustache,
on a painting he's told he better
admire.

          Whatever, time and time,
its moistures, its rusts,
have lent a hand, have blotted
this and bloodied that.

                    And now
like some mute if ominous mystery
they stand.
                    As with an ancient folk
that all its life had nothing to say
for itself, nothing but the poverty
that fell on it, the hardships
and the crises, chartless desert
they passed through.
                    And yet,
its many a mark on them like dignity,
badges, they did. And no one could
deny them.

The Little Red Book

to that "great poet," President Mao Tse-tung

At last a little book
to replace all other books
as though it had, swallowing them,
digested into perfect, obvious wisdom.

For a poet wrote it, a mighty
poet, who withdrew all his other
works from circulation. And now
all the people, China itself, live

by this book, a text
holier, they believe, than Buddha,
Laotse, or Wang Wei for telling
whatever one has to know.

It is as though Rimbaud,
forsaking poetry, had turned
to propaganda, revolution, war
instead of slave traffic and gun-

running, as though
his genius had found a medium

nothing else could equal: people.
And at last his will, complying

with his deepest wish,
was magic to change the world.
The change is such that at any time
a million million people

are turning like a million
million leaves on a mammoth tree
to one strong wind, maybe Wang Wei's
friendly, well-groved, walnut tree,

but tending raptures
rather different from those
that Wang Wei had in mind, turning
to one page and to one precept,

all the people of China
turning like one and into one
as they repeat in certain unison
the only true, all-sufficient words.

A Very Tokyo

You threw in the magazine.
Its cover billowing, flames page
by page reviewed it that the fire
was itself impressed. And we?
Warmed too like bystanders

enjoying the crackle
and the animation, arms flailing
away, of a talk they cannot
catch the meaning of, then slowly,
arm in arm, the speakers dis-

appearing in the twilight.
For some time after, though dark
looked more and more through
puffy embers, the glamor of that
conversation sparkled up and down

our minds, some few words
flying still, fat ashy birds
out of a night-bedoubled stand
of trees. It is all folded many
times over like our little Japan-

ese maple that is wrapt up
in its foliage. We wonder how
for such huge crowd, a very Tokyo,
it breathes. It's no surprise
the leaves must keep such quiet

and such deep-down privacy
until a sudden breeze combines
them like a single bell, one many-
mouthed sigh, one fire roaring
through that horde of words.

Those acts and feelings,
imperturbables in their need
that we can scarcely understand,
in a moment's blazon which they
bear, grow lightning-plain.

The Rage to Live

All day I groped
in my mind for the kind
of image that would get close
to you.
       And I saw you,
steeped in your juices,
like a whale in its wallow,
big enough
       in its terrible
lurch to be its own world,
a world. But even that
seemed a little
       shallow.
So I slipped from that
to an image of the sea itself,
fairly calm
       at the moment,
yet soon enough a seismic
tidal wave, and I retreating,
afraid
       to bring my boat
too near lest you, sweeping it
up, in its fragility make
its cargo too much
       to bear.

But this also, far as it went,
had to fail. I saw it was
in your nature,
                your nature's
being true to itself,
to wreck them all. And
only then I got
                a salty whiff
of what might work. I saw
that it took the oldest
and the best
                to know you.
I must catch me a sea-beast
and, flaying it, crouch down
inside its fat,
                hot, stinking
hide and wait there, wait
between near retching,
hunger, love,
                stiff pride.
And finally, when you appear
to gather in this other
of your flock
                for the having,
I must leap out, grip you,
not let go though you whip
into every
                massive self
you are, slip through my hands,
mag-dog-glistening water,
writhe, a snake
                of fire,
and all the rest until at last
the shape round back on you
that knows you best.
                And there—
the beasts and the elements

like skins sloughed behind,
the wind reveling
                    through,
for all the stink those cast-
off skins have made one seared
yet soaring scent—
                    the image,
sea that's everywhere a shore,
finds me, neither of us
yet both, our anchor, core.

A Place of Blood

Maybe there was nothing
real about it in the first place,
this story that they told, first told
as well in a place and a time we now
cannot establish.
                    Nonetheless,
they gathered round it like black,
nattering crows, beaked for victims
and a juicy morsel, cawing, beaking,
till they fell
                    upon each other,
and the sky puffed up with flying
feathers like a great, slow snowfall,
bedabbled by a bloody tumult. There-
after there were markers
                    of a sort
to indicate something had happened,
something grim, therefore engrossing,
something the race could turn to
in disaster as in joy.
                    And because
the hordes were for it, brought
their interest with their children,
dropped their garbage, took home
facts of their own making,

                        the story
has grown true and truer. Who's
to say that, when the generations
have stamped a certain spot down,
stamped and fallen there
                        past all
account by one stroke or another,
such a story has not found the way
to suck out of whatever happens
strength and sweetness grounding it.

Conservation: American Style

for Erich Kahler

Innocent as he was,
this American conservationist,
with his huge hands and his earnestness,
he proved a most attractive traveling
companion.
          Dutifully with a sober
enthusiasm he visited all the shrines.
But finally in Sardinia even he broke down.
And then he said to you unforgettably,
"Some day soon
              you must come
to Kansas, especially my part of it.
There you'd never be bothered by tourists."
Later you learned, when he ignored
the two elegant,
            altogether lovable
Peruvians who shared your table,
that he had fallen in love with a terrible
Ecuadorian. Maybe, having lived in Kansas
all his life,
        he needed that kind

of excitement, needed to feel like a shrine
overrun by noisy, trampling tourists,
at other times to be as vast
and empty as the plains of Kansas.

The Youngest Son

Cast out among your impatient,
scornful elders: the first a scholar
hunched over his books in several languages
before you learned to say "May I";

the second quick, clever
at finding your clumsiness like dirt
all over your body; and your many sisters,
grim, raw, willed like jealous men.

With your wiry little father
forever in the mood of fire, a single
word enough to flare him forth, exacting
instantaneous obedience from his stiff brood,

treating you like some mistake
his wife unforgivably had made. Soon
you learned the skills of skulking, hiding,
stealing. Hard-handed words, blows

aimed at one's weaknesses,
mold one as well as any other lesson.
You became, perfect, exactly what they said
you were, a cheat, a thief, a liar.

And yet they found you
useful for the minor, dingy chores.
You brought in water and wood, swept floors,
carried messages, often those

most revealing since they
hardly cared about your knowing.
Maybe it was then you started, broom in hand
and shears, some flowers, of a Sunday

to take care of the family
plot, tending graves of brothers
and sisters who had barely lived, some dying
many years before your birth.

Then, grown up, you went
about your business, from one job
and trouble to another, your second brother
most exasperatedly bailing you out,

the whole family meeting
to recount your failures or, worse,
to sit over you in brooding, stony silence.
Still no matter how far you wandered

you could not let them go.
And reluctantly they accepted what
they thought was your dependence, weakness
natural to such a ne'er-do-well.

Now age has come upon them.
The oldest, more bent than ever,
recognizes no one. Only you can reach him,
feed him; only you are there

below his books. So one
by one they turn to you, efficient—

for the arts you've learned—in the larger,
necessary chores. You, the cheat,

the thief, the liar,
come of age at last. Your training
they were all so set on giving now works
splendidly. And you move among them.

Having been a child of trouble
all your life, you take the family over.

Pleasure, Pleasure

And watching Hoppy curled up
in my lap, the way he goes
purring under my hand into sleep,
this watching is a pleasure.

A pleasure too Renée
in the next room practicing
the violin, going over the same
tracks again and again, trying

the notes like doors
to stores more and more open
for business, like stars lighting
up some Persian night asleep

under the skin of day.
Is a pleasure and a pleasure
this friend and that, a light
of one color and another,

not only to read
by as the world takes shape,
the sea rolled over like Hoppy
in a rapture of churning,

but a light
that is also the thing lit,
the world in its juicy, joyous
particulars. And outside the day

in each leaf now
is lighting, each leaf by its own
lights, maple first, then sumac,
inspired but responding as it

has to. Already
the year is more than half way
here, to be followed by snow
throwing itself like a confetti,

going up and then,
to go farther, down in a very
ecstasy of windy cold. Pleasure,
pleasure and the darkest light.

Stoneward

As though one pried
under the lids of faces
in old pictures (this, for
instance, framed in clothes

a little quaint now,
admitting nothing of the
fact that one among the set
is bent on madness ripening),

broke the rigid lids
of ancient statues, especially
those already of themselves
full-bodied monsters,

and saw reflected
in them sights reptilian
enough, still squirming on,
to turn one into stone.

In dreams sometimes,
when the whole head opens
like a giant lid, the mind
become one unblinking eye,

those creatures and the sights,
their necessary landscapes,
emerge as though from caves,
from under flaming rocks,

and for some time-
less moment we are locked
in a world, stars crackling
round us, the ancients saw

enough of to avert
by stoning over the eyes—
joys too are such disguise—
of their most daring deities.

The Last Letters,

whether they be followed
by what we call a natural death
or suicide, tend to be the most engrossing.

A certain amount of excitement,
sensationalism even, attaches to them.
But that's real enough and not to be denied,

a kind of undressing
so complete nothing else can possibly compare.
Beyond that, as we lean closer,

squinting at the lines,
we have the sense of drawing near
not only the most, but the ultimate of living;

for here, whatever the strength
of the occasion and the affectations,
not to say disingenuousness, death may induce,

a man, precisely
as he turns his back on what
he has been thirty years or seventy, is bound,

as much as he ever can,
to tell the truth. And turns his back as well
on all the future, as though to say

not all its promises
can make him tarry; that or what
he's in for, he now knows, can only grow worse,

the emptiness, the deprivation,
worst if he's been happy. And even if nothing
more than nothing should ensue,

the void ("he took his dog
for its evening walk, then shot
his brains out" or "she set out her rare plant

to catch the rain,
made several phone calls, and downed
an overdose of pills"), something must crackle

over that last broken line,
something, we cannot help feeling,
from the other side, of that life even as it

is being consumed,
even as it consumes itself forever
in its own private flame, now breaking loose,

like some great moth
throwing itself into the fire
that is itself to enlarge it, but lost to it

in the very moment of having.
And most of all if it is someone who has been
a success. As we say, a great gift,

gifts he finally admits
of no help to him, a burden rather.
Surely something immense for him to be willing

to—or have to—abandon them.
As if to say we also, whatever love we've felt
for him, did not find his gifts enough.

Not till now.

The Second Time

I read your words again
in hope there might be meanings
I had missed, sights, a taste
of honey hanging from the underside
this later light helps to remark.

Maybe the words this time
will join in acts they did not
care to carry out; maybe my need,
now shifted some, will summon
from them sympathy, amusement,

slumbering before, as sun
surprises this thick-berried bush,
slow leaf by leaf, in drawing off.
The power, I am sure, was there
from the beginning but in repose

and waiting for the hunger
capable of deserving it. A little
like a walk one takes in streets,
tree-lined, the time say autumn,
a neighborhood one knows by heart.

But changes have been going
on, startling in the way they
underline the old, changes changing as one passes them for the late
hour, the light's peculiar slant.

And tinted too by the mood
one brings, the shadows
falling, oneself the interloper
or at least the drama ruffling
the leaves in passing. And suddenly

as blood unheralded may stream
from a mouth that spoke calm,
familiar phrases, the dark exudes
from the sky but also from these
trees and bushes till you wonder

whether your own eyelids are
not shedding it. And now the last
word like the hand of someone
turning a far corner, lingering
the light, bids "good night."

The Watermark

At the end
like a wet moth caught—
how gloriously it poured all that
night—in a nook of soaked grasses

you wrote, wrote
letters to all, to the dead
as to the living, to those you had
heard and never heard of,

those perfect ones
yet to be, having to struggle
through countless dates and bodies
before they would dare

the term of flesh.
Maybe now that the truth
at last was in you, the truth
roaring as it ripped through you,

maybe now someone
would hear, someone would have
the kind of listening to complete—
so quiet and fix forever—that truth.

Like a spider
you wrote glittering lines out
everywhere, and your life was there,
felt everywhere along them,

like a many-
handed sea-creature emitting
a deluge of ink. At the end
they found you, the pen clutched

in your hand,
a crumpled sheet of paper
before you, but, the watermark
drying, not one word written on it.

A Walk in the Forest

The postcard must be from you;
I recognize your handwriting
in my address, though the return
is much less legible.
                    The view
might be Vallombrosa or at least
a walk through a most considerate
forest, its waterfall
                    a modest
ghost in one corner or maybe
a stare that has not yet focused,
a moment
            in the timelessness—
and that moment become timeless—
of the Garden. But the writing
on the back,
                though it marches
along in no uncertain lines
that say it knows what it is
saying,
            is meaningless to me,
for its accents the handiwork
of some entirely unknown person,
a little like
                turning a corner

of a familiar city and suddenly
entering a brandnew spot. And then
(brimmed, is it,
                    from the view?)
all that blueness, as though
the sky were taller here than most
airs could accommodate.
                              So I try
to read you over and over, not
to understand but to take in
part of you
                    to make one moment
and one coming along somewhat later—
a postponed delivery—connected,
continuous, even possible.

Needlepoint

You wove the moth
into your tapestry, of stuffs
that must have spun straight
out of its belly,
               silks
that bulked around it, over,
clouds puffy-cheeked like gods
nestled in soft,
               lofty clover.
Meantime, that very Shelley
of a nightingale warbled out
its song, dark
               it clustered,
seen from a sunny, daisy point-
of-view. Smells too as they
would materialize
               for eye
and finger to enjoy; and tucked
inside the curled-out grass,
knots of weeds
               and tussocks
peepers might seem the piping
of, you eked out toothsome
worms below
               to counterpoint

the moth above, as though, so
contained, turned into a heavenly sight,
        like cherubim
they would be humming hymns.
Winds, blowing through, ruffled
in fancy stitches,
             knew that
they were eased into something
flutes might play, a catch
forever in the thrum.
            Forever
till the moth, the worms,
munching away, eat the winds,
the gods, the scene, each other.

A Public Life

*"Ever since a Boy I have had an astonishing
desire to see much of the World and particularly
to acquire a true knowledge of the Birds..."*
                                    AUDUBON

What discrimination!
According to his own carefully kept
record he knew at least a thousand women,
and of course quite a few young girls,
not to forget a man and a boy or so.

And what a medley
of rooms and beds he made his way
through, set on preparing the perfect
Baedecker. Hard at work night and day,
no Audubon pinned his birds

better, wings spread
to the full, all their colors
on display, that array of private
parts brighter yet for his intent look
fixed on them. Thus he remembers—

though he gave them,
it seems, so ruthlessly was he

devoted to his course, hardly more time
than the rest—remembers loving
a certain two.

He does his best
to say what it was about them
won his love, and he is graphic enough.
Yet vivid details and all, I doubt
that any outsider could tell

them much apart
from the nine hundred ninety-eight
others. But why be surprised before one
who gladly sacrificed all else to this
priestly career he carried on

most of his life.
Surely with an interest like his
he could make the subtlest distinctions.
What is truly astonishing however
and much more revealing is that

out of the midst
of such a crowd he could think
to call his account *My Secret Life*!
That when it is his long public life
we know far less about.

A Fitting Revenge

For seeing you naked
you turned his own pack
on him.
        You needn't have
bothered. After one glimpse
of you
        he would have
spurned all women—"a sight
like that,
          heart itself
leaped to a spot of its own
it never
        knew before,
what falling back?"—do you
require worship
             greater
than that? Or, even better,
set as he was
         for keeps
on recovering that moment's
vision,
        he would have tried
to climb over them all,
so many foothills
           of a giant

mountain. And if at times
he fell back
            and in a cave,
some moss-lined recess
of the mountain—
                  "I thought
I might hide a little
from the blast
            of lightning
stuck in my eyes, looking
or shut;
            let it be a shadow,
I said, to shield me from
her golden rain"—
                  loitered
to drink of a lesser spring,
be sure the taste
                  would be
most bitter, your face
lucid, mocking
                  as he bent
to drink, and he would spit
it out,
            bitten enough—
he goading—by his own mad,
ravenous dogs.
            Surely
you know, and no one better,
no other meat tastes
                  sweet—
none so hunger-breeding—
as a man's eating his own.

A Certain Village

Once in late summer,
the road already deep in twilight,
mixing colors with some straggly
wildflowers, I came to a village
I did not know was there
                          until
I stepped into its narrow street.
Admiring the prim, white houses
nestled among their battered,
lofty trees,
            I found myself in
a tiny square with a little dawdl-
ing fountain and a rickety tower,
its owlish clock absentmindedly
counting minutes now and then.

And in the fountain the face
of morning seemed to linger as
though searching. The air was fresh,
breathing out the fragrances
of a recent shower.
                    I luxuriated
in my senses, like meeting
unexpectedly a pack of friends

years and years unthought of, laden
with all kinds of gifts.
                    Then
as I stopped to knock at the door
of a house that had seemed occupied
with happy noises, a silence
fell on it,
                the light went out—
and was it instant eyes like flakes,
ten thousand, thousand flakes,
and all unknowing, flurried
round me?
                Wherever I turned
I was met by the unmistakable
accusation, "Stranger!" I, who had,
I thought, begun here and who now
required lodgings
                    for the night,
was denied and from the start.